# ANTIQUE FURNITURE
by Nova Scotian Craftsmen

No. 1. A corner of the parlour at Uniacke House, Mount Uniacke, Hants County.
PHOTO COURTESY OF NOVA SCOTIA FILM BUREAU.

# ANTIQUE FURNITURE
## by Nova Scotian Craftsmen

### GEORGE E. G. MacLAREN

ADVISORY EDITOR:

### PHYLLIS R. BLAKELEY

Foreword by LORNE PIERCE

## McGRAW-HILL RYERSON LIMITED
Toronto   Montreal   New York   London   Sydney   Johannesburg
Mexico   Panama   Düsseldorf   Singapore   Sao Paulo
Kuala Lumpur   New Delhi   Auckland

ISBN 0-07-077706-3

2 3 4 5 6 7 8 9 10  JD  75 4 3 2 1 0 9 8

PRINTED AND BOUND IN CANADA

*To My Father*

EDWARD MARSHALL MacLAREN
Pictou, N.S.
1871 - 1946

# ACKNOWLEDGMENTS

In the preparation of this work I have been helped very greatly by Miss Phyllis Blakeley, Assistant Archivist of Nova Scotia, whose extensive knowledge of the history of the province has been brought to the reading and editing of the manuscript.

The Public Archives of Nova Scotia's collection of manuscripts, newspapers and histories provided the main source for research in this field, and I wish to thank Dr. C. B. Fergusson for permission to consult them.

The Provincial Museum's collection of photographs of Nova Scotian crafts and furniture by Mr. Edward Longard of the Museum staff and by Mr. Robert Jones and Mr. William Wood brings before the reader for the first time the era in which design and the skill of the craftsman in this province reached an excellence that has never been surpassed.

My thanks are due to Mr. Ross G. Graves of West Gore, Hants County, for information on the Cole family, and to the Rev. Kennedy Wainwright of Stewiacke, Colchester County, for his research on the Sibley family of Wittenburg. I have received much inspiration from the paper prepared by the late Mrs. Florence Belcher Payzant on "Old Furniture Made in Nova Scotia" and read before the Antiquarian Club of Halifax on February 28, 1939.

The encouragement of Dr. Lorne Pierce of Toronto has provided the incentive that led towards the completion of this work. To the many friends who have placed their collections and knowledge at my disposal, I am most grateful.

GEORGE E. G. MacLAREN

*Halifax, Nova Scotia,*
*September, 1961.*

# FOREWORD

This is the first attempt to record the history of one of the native handcrafts in the Maritime Provinces. Books, brochures and miscellaneous articles have referred to Maritime handcrafts, but they have been tentative and casual at best. Whatever has been done in cabinetmaking and silver, in ceramics and glass elsewhere in Canada has been done with equal distinction in the Maritime Provinces.

This book is the first full and formal account of Maritime cabinetmaking, and is exclusively concerned with Nova Scotia. Others may now complete the record by covering New Brunswick and Prince Edward Island. Moreover, the present book is only a fragment of the author's full study of native crafts in Nova Scotia. In time it is to be hoped that Mr. George MacLaren will round out the series with monographs on Nova Scotian glass, pottery, stoves and architecture.

A fascinating book could have been written long ago on Maritime figureheads, those heroic, gaily painted wood-carvings that once graced the prows of sailing vessels made and manned and sailed round the world from the sheltering coves of those Maritime Provinces. But these wood carvings of Poseidon, Atalanta, Britannia and other tutelary deities whose home was the ocean sea—they have gone. Some went down with their ships in far deep waters, some on reefs along the Atlantic coast, and others wasted away in many a Nova Scotia cove waiting for masters and schooners and cargoes that never came. Only a few survive.

As in all the provinces of Canada, predatory antique dealers and other hunters raided the Maritime Provinces, and priceless things, in vast quantities, were lugged away and sold to the gullible as Early Rhode Island, Antique Vermont and so on. Only now are we waking up after our long sleep of neglect.

Though much has been ravished and plundered, much remains. Private collectors in Canada will, upon reading George MacLaren's book, seek out and preserve whatever is left, for these things are priceless symbols of our industrial and cultural beginnings. Government appropriations to our museums and archives should be marked with imagination and courage. This book holds up a light showing the way to what must be done.

*Antique Furniture by Nova Scotian Craftsmen* is well planned. It traces the principal sources of immigration, and shows what skills the various nationalities brought with them. Next, we are given an outline of the general cultural life of the Maritime Provinces, its main characteristics by regions: Lunenburg, Yarmouth, Chignecto, Halifax, Pictou and so on. Over against this background we have a hint of the distinguished work going on in all the Maritime Provinces, in furniture, silver, glass, pottery, clockmaking, and carriage making.

"Cabinetmakers and Their Woods" is an ideal approach to the general theme of this book. First they took the wood nearest and cheapest, pine, maple, birch and cherry, utility keeping pace with more professional work in design and finish. Beyond the four principal native woods the Maritime artisan had to reach out to the walnut of New England and the mahogany of the Caribbean. These imported woods were symbols of luxury and status, as well as of increasing pride and skill in the craft of furniture making.

The author pays special attention to the types of furniture that were most commonly in use. "Chairs and Their Makers" introduces us to types important enough to be listed in detail in inventories of estates, and gives us the names of the aristocracy among the makers, the three generations of the Cole family, for example, and Sibley. The types run from the unpainted pine chair, scrubbed until it looked like white satin, to the carved mahogany seats of the mighty in the Legislative Council chamber of Nova Scotia. "Furniture Factories" is the proud record of Stephen, Gordon, Keith, and Cumming, and the wide variety of their products, running from kitchen chairs to church pews, sofas, cradles, beds, chests and cupboards. So the story goes, including clocks and pianofortes, and ending up with, quite properly, "The Romance of Collecting Furniture." The rich profusion of illustrations permits us to see some of the prize pieces that survive in Nova Scotia, and they are enough to make any province proud. To round out the record, the author has provided an Appendix in which he assembles the names of companies and craftsmen, with localities and dates. This is very important, both for authenticating examples of early furniture, and as offering clues for collectors in their hunt for such treasures as remain, hidden in attics and otherwise forgotten or ignored.

George MacLaren deserves the special thanks both of his province and of museums and collectors everywhere. Born in historic Pictou County, and with Maritime tradition in his bones, he has been in government service in Nova Scotia for thirty years, and for the last six years has been Curator of the Nova Scotia Museum, Historical section, at Citadel Hill, Halifax. He is a graduate of the School of Fine Arts and Crafts, Boston, a four year course, and was a student of crafts and furniture in Florence for a year.

The Historical Museum collections range over the usual wide field: furniture, silver, coins, glass, ceramics, paintings, crafts, agricultural implements and so on.

There were no reference works and little else to go on, therefore the Curator had to find his own way—the long, still hunt. The field for research in all the categories represented in the collections is still wide open. Mr. MacLaren's personal explorations and finds have been tentatively summed up in his vast manuscript, with illustrations, chiefly concerned with ceramics, stoves, wood-carving and silver. To date he has published *Nova Scotia Museum Newsletter* (April, 1958) on early Nova Scotian Glass, and *The Pictou Book* (New Glasgow, 1954), a history of the first settlements in Pictou County. Nothing of any consequence has been written about Nova Scotian furniture making outside the province. Three recent publications deal professionally with early furniture: *The Canadian Collector,* by Gerald Stevens (author of *Early Canadian Glass* and other works), deals with cabinetmaking in early Ontario and Quebec (Toronto, Ryerson, 1957); *The Furniture of French Canada,* by F. St. George Spendlove, F.R.G.S., Curator of Canadiana Collections, the Royal Ontario Museum (R.O.M., 1954); *Collectors' Luck,* by F. St. George Spendlove, deals with clocks, Canadian and foreign, French Canadian furniture, Regency style in Canadian furniture, and Chinese style in European furniture of the eighteenth century (Toronto, Ryerson, 1960).

Having been born in a family of cabinetmakers, and being interested in this craft from his earliest years, George MacLaren has been able to recognize a good thing when he sees it, and sometimes to wheedle the owner into letting him have it. For the most part he has had to stand aside and watch old families selling their treasures, some of it passing on to heirs who had no love for it, or to dealers who loved it in a much different way. Now and then he has had the rare thrill that comes to all real collectors some time in their lives, as for example the discovery of a Tulles, Pallister and M'Donald grandfather clock made in Halifax in 1810, and being able to secure it for the Museum. He has persuaded young married people to collect before everything ends up in the United States or Upper Canada Village.

Remembering his grandfather, born in 1836, and his father, born in 1873, and remembering, too, their tales of old times; recalling the craftsmen of his home town, the last of the local carriagemakers, tinsmiths, saddlemakers, cabinetmakers, and shoemakers, all at work in their small shops and factories, George MacLaren would harvest everything worthwhile that remains into his growing collections for the delight of those who follow after. His great regret is that his son can never share in those adventures he once so much enjoyed, silently watching the last of the Nova Scotia pioneer craftsmen at their painstaking task. In the Nova Scotia Museum all Canadians may renew their pride in those master craftsmen who had so much to do with laying the foundation of an authentic native culture in Nova Scotia.

LORNE PIERCE

# CONTENTS

# KEY TO THE APPENDICES

# LIST OF ILLUSTRATIONS

❦ CHAPTER ONE

# The Pioneers and Their Crafts

A forgotten group in every community when history comes to record the greatness of its men and women are the craftsmen whose skills have helped to shape a way of life.

When our forefathers crossed the Atlantic in small sailing vessels to make their homes in the New World they had to bring their food and bedding, for in those days no luxuriously furnished staterooms and dining saloons were provided for passengers. The cargo would include tools and seeds, supplies for the long winter, clothing and blankets for their new homes, but not expensive furniture. Chests containing clothes and blankets, spinning wheels, looms and tools were the nearest approach to furniture brought by the pioneers.

### THE ACADIANS

The first white men to come to the Maritime Provinces with the expectation of making a permanent settlement were Sieur de Monts, Poutrincourt, Samuel de Champlain and their company of one hundred and twenty artisans, labourers and soldiers who built shelters on an island in the St. Croix River in 1604. A cold winter proved that this was an unsatisfactory site, and the next summer most of the buildings were taken down and transported in the little ships to Port Royal on the shore of the beautiful Annapolis Basin.

There these Frenchmen built for their Habitation, with "fair sawn timbers," as close a replica of a sixteenth-century French manor house as they could. They were the only Europeans living in North America, and the forest

1

stretched southwards without a break from Nova Scotia to Florida. Here Samuel de Champlain originated the *Ordre de Bon Temps* to keep the men amused during the long winter, and here Marc Lescarbot wrote and produced the first play in North America, which he called the *Theatre of Neptune*.

In 1613, when Acadia became a battleground between France and England, the Port Royal Habitation was burned by Captain Samuel Argall from Virginia. It was restored in 1939-1940, however, local residents being employed as workmen. Several of these had been ships' carpenters who could use whipsaw, adze and broadaxe with dexterity and had a feeling for wood.

Research has not shown that any qualified cabinetmakers accompanied the French to Nova Scotia in 1604. The task of making furniture would fall to shipwrights, coopers and carpenters. In the Habitation we may see the types of simple furniture used by the early French settlers: substantial tables of hewn wood, benches, straight-backed chairs, bunks and sea chests. Floors were covered with the skins of animals.

The kings of France and their ministers left the destinies of Acadia in the hands of adventurers and traders. Most of the Acadian people living in the Maritime Provinces today are descended from the three hundred French settlers who were brought out by Isaac de Razilly and D'Aulnay Charnisay from 1632 to 1640. These Acadians were farmers and fishermen, with a few blacksmiths and carpenters. The population grew slowly; in 1671 there were only 441 people in Acadia, 363 of them living at Port Royal. After 1710 the Acadians had small settlements at Minas, Grand Pré, Piziquid (now Windsor), Cobequid (now Truro), and at Beaubassin and Chignecto (near the present site of Amherst).

Acadia under French rule, having but a small population, was never an important administrative centre like Quebec. There was no Bishop Laval to bring to Acadia wood-carvers, designers and craftsmen, or to further production. There were no *châteaux* and *manoirs* in Acadia to call for Louis XIV furniture, no corrupt and wealthy officials like Indendant Bigot who could afford Louis XV furnishings.

When Gargas, who had been appointed principal clerk, visited Port Royal in 1687, he reported that all the houses were low, made of rough pieces of wood, one on top of another, and roofed with thatch. Only the governor's residence was covered with planks. Gargas urged the French authorities to supply the soldiers and settlers with tools, "none of them having money to buy tools." Half a century later, Abbé Maillard said that there were practically no craftsmen in the country, but that the inhabitants built their own homes and that "with a plane and knife, an Acadian would build his house and barn, and even make all his wooden domestic furniture."

No. 2. Acadian grandfather and grandmother chairs at the Dugas house in Clare.
PHOTO BY E. G. L. WETMORE.

Ceded to England in 1713, Acadia had increased in population from two thousand to nearly ten thousand by 1755. In that year and in the years following, English-speaking soldiers burned thousands of dwellings and barns in the Acadian villages, and deported nearly six thousand Acadians to the thirteen American colonies along the Atlantic coast. Some escaped to what is now New Brunswick and Prince Edward Island, or lived in the forest with the assistance of the Indians.

When France and England made peace again in 1763, the government of Nova Scotia permitted the Acadians to return. Some came back to their native land by ships from the southern colonies, from St. Pierre, and from Quebec. One group of nine hundred trekked through the wilderness from Boston to the Annapolis valley. There they discovered that their old farms had been occupied by English-speaking strangers, and they were forced to clear new land for themselves at Clare in Digby County. Others settled along the south shore at Pubnico, at Tracadie in Antigonish County, and in Cape Breton Island on Isle Madame and at Cheticamp (later to become famous for its hooked rugs).

The old Acadian furniture has been destroyed by fire, and little remains of that which belonged to the Acadian pioneers who returned to Nova Scotia in the 1760's and 1770's. Some may be seen in the Acadian Room at the Fort Anne Museum in Annapolis Royal, and there are old Acadian grandfather and grandmother chairs in the Dugas house at Grosses Coques, Digby County.

### THE FIRST HALIGONIANS

From the day of its founding in 1749 as a base against the French at Louisbourg and Quebec, Halifax was both the capital and the chief centre of Nova Scotia. Located on a magnificent ice-free harbour, it has been the seat of government, headquarters of the army, base for the navy, and principal port for passenger and merchant shipping. Its fortunes have risen with war and fallen with peace; but at no time, except during the brief brilliance of Shelburne, has it had any rival in population or wealth. In Halifax, therefore, there grew up a class of officers, officials and wealthy merchants who had sufficient money, leisure and interest to afford the amenities of social life and the advantages of culture, and who were able to import expensive furniture from abroad and to patronize local cabinetmakers.

When Governor Edward Cornwallis arrived at Halifax in June 1749 with about 2,500 English settlers, he found trees growing to the water's edge. Under his direction a town was built on the western shore of the harbour by the British soldiers and by Cockneys unaccustomed to such toil. A large piece of ground was cleared in six weeks, and then divided among the new inhabitants by lots. Each man had to construct his own shelter, with the assistance of his family and friends, for carpenters and bricklayers were not available. The British government provided boards and shingles and nails, which arrived by sloop from Boston.

One observer commented: "Many of the English built very poor houses, and many of them none at all, being incapable of such business, and therefore were obliged to shelter themselves all the winter in their tents." Food was plentiful in the new town, but clothing was scarce and expensive, and the writer advised any friends planning to come to Nova Scotia to "bring no money, but tapes, thread, stockings, linen &c for they will double the value."

Edward Draper, who arrived on the ship *Winchelsea*, is the first cabinetmaker to emigrate to Nova Scotia of whom we have record. He is the only cabinetmaker listed among those who accompanied Cornwallis to Halifax. As little furniture, other than chests, had been brought from the mother country, it fell to those most skilled in general handicraft, including fourteen joiners and three turners who had come with Cornwallis' fleet (see Appendix C), to knock together makeshifts of the type commonly found in English cottages. These amateurs made rough plank tables and chairs with rush-bottomed seats. Wealthy officials and military men such as Richard Bulkeley would import some furniture from Boston and from England. William Craft, upholsterer, came on the *Winchelsea* in 1749, and was still in Halifax in 1752.

The only piece of furniture surviving from the days of the founding of Halifax is Cornwallis' table, which may be seen in the Red Chamber in Province House. This is an oak table brought from England, and His Majesty's Council for the Province of Nova Scotia sat around it on board the transport *Beaufort* in Halifax Harbour on July 14, 1749. It is a long table with six legs on ball feet, and the stretchers around the outside and across the middle bear the mark of booted feet.

Most of the English who came to live in Nova Scotia settled at Halifax, as did many men discharged from the army and navy. In the 1770's, before the outbreak of the American Revolution, several hundred Yorkshire families settled on the vacant Acadian lands at Chignecto, near Fort Beauséjour, in what is now Westmorland and Cumberland Counties, where the towns of Dorchester, Sackville and Amherst now flourish. They were substantial farmers who had left Yorkshire because of high rents. They had money to buy and stock farms in Nova Scotia, and they brought some farm equipment and essential household furnishings from England.

### THE "FOREIGN PROTESTANTS"

At the time of the founding of Halifax the authorities in England did not encourage emigration from the British Isles. Yet more settlers were needed in Nova Scotia. The government sent agents to Europe to recruit Protestants who were willing to make new homes across the Atlantic. These agents were paid a guinea a head for each settler they secured, so it is not surprising to hear of some agents who persuaded the emigrants to sell all their household possessions in order to pack more people on the ships.

The majority of these "Foreign Protestants" were from the provinces bordering the Rhine River and the German part of Switzerland, but hundreds were French-speaking Protestants from Montbeliard and Switzerland. By 1753 over two thousand "Foreign Protestants" had arrived in Halifax, where they were nicknamed "Dutch" from the German *Deutsch*. Indian raids making it impossible for these people to go into the country to farm, about fifteen hundred of them were sent in June 1753 to found the town of Lunenburg. There they continued to suffer great hardships, until peace was made with the Indians in 1760 and they could move into the surrounding country to make new homes.

The blockhouses and barracks of the struggling pioneer town of Lunenburg were places of refuge and defence, and apparently also maternity hospitals. Twenty-six cradles were available in the year 1759, when ninety-eight

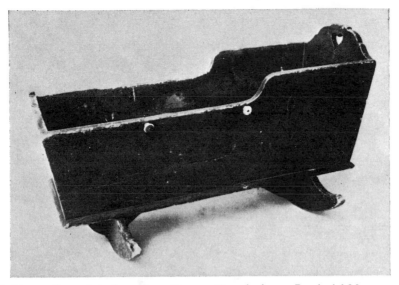

No. 3. Pine cradle made in Lunenburg County. Note the heart. Provincial Museum, Citadel Hill, Halifax. PHOTO BY E. LONGARD.

No. 4. Mahogany cradle used by Henry Pope Mulhall (born September 9, 1850) of Liverpool, Queens County. Presented to the Public Archives of Nova Scotia by his daughter, Mrs. Edith Mulhall Achilles of New York. PHOTO BY ROBERT JONES.

births took place at the various barracks. The Lunenburg cradles were solidly built, with pine sides, ends, bottoms and rockers, and were painted to suit the taste of the owners.

The Germans brought with them trunks, bedding, pewter and iron pots, tools, churns, spinning wheels, and perhaps some equipment for farming. The stock of the first store in Lunenburg is said to have been kept in a trunk made of heavy birch plank and filled with calicoes, ribbons, needles and other goods sent from Halifax by her sisters to Mrs. Martin Born. In the early days of Lunenburg most furniture would have been made by handymen and carpenters, working from their recollections of furniture left at home. Not a single cabinetmaker was listed on the passenger lists of the "Foreign Protestants" coming to Nova Scotia from 1750 to 1753, but there were thirty-five joiners. (See Appendix D.)

Those settlers speaking German remained in or near Lunenburg, gradually expanding over the whole county, while the French-speaking ones moved to the North-west Range, to St. Margaret's Bay, to Tatamagouche and River John. Retaining their customs and their language for more than a century, the Germans gave Lunenburg County a distinctive tradition and culture.

Although the poll tax lists of the 1790's contain the name of only one cabinetmaker (Alexander McNeal) in Lunenburg County, the proportion of carpenters, shipcarpenters, turners and wheelwrights was higher there than in other districts, and any of these men could make furniture. For instance, Casper Jung (Young) was listed in 1794 as a turner and wheelwright, and in 1795 as a wheelwright in Lunenburg town. In 1927, the late Harry Piers acquired for the Nova Scotia Museum of Science a small spinning wheel made by Mr. Young of Martin's River or Mahone Bay, Lunenburg County, who constructed many spinning wheels used in that county. It was used for spinning flax and occasionally wool.

When William Moorsom, a captain in the 52nd Light Infantry Regiment stationed in the garrison at Halifax, visited Lunenburg about 1828, he praised the neatness of the brightly painted wooden houses and other buildings of Lunenburg County, a characteristic still remarked by visitors. The homes of Lunenburg town contained "old German Clocks, and Dutch chimney-

No. 5. Spinning wheel, made by F. Young of Lunenburg County about 1835, in the collection of H. E. Dawes, Ottawa, Ontario.

ornaments; chairs of a mould as substantial as wood can form, and heavy-colored pictures . . . while the fine Axminster carpet, polished sofa-table, and full festooned window-drapery, appear like innovating usurpers of ancient demesne, conscious of their power. . . ."

Captain Moorsom's complaints about the temperature of the country cottages and about the feather beds are typical of English army officers. "The close German stove is universally employed to convert the room into a sort

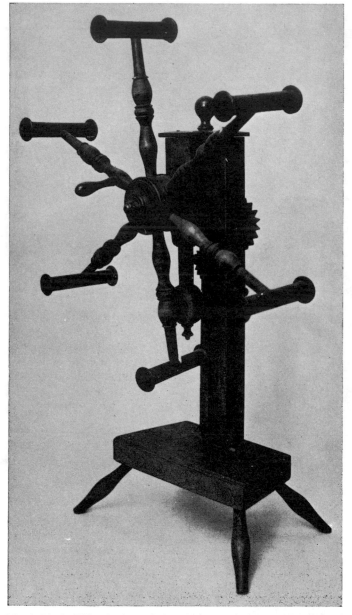

No. 6. Birch click-wheel or skein winder made by A. McIntosh of Pictou County about 1830.    At Provincial Museum, Citadel Hill, Halifax.    PHOTO BY E. LONGARD.

of oven, almost suffocating to those who have not by long habit been baked to the same temperature and consistence as the natives. Sometimes also the German bed puzzles the untravelled visitor whose acuteness is rarely sufficient to direct him to an interval between two mountains of feathers, as the place assigned for his corporeal refreshment, after a broiling summer's day."

In their homeland the Lunenburgers were a people of the soil. In Nova Scotia their environment forced them to learn shipbuilding and navigation, the only way to transport their produce to Halifax was by sea, and the fishing grounds off the coast were a tempting source of food. By the beginning of the nineteenth century Lunenburgers were already at home on the sea, and shipbuilding and fishing were bringing prosperity to the south shore.

### THE NEW ENGLANDERS

The expulsion of the Acadians left empty and desolate some of the richest and pleasantest lands in Nova Scotia. In the 1760's about five thousand New Englanders came to the Annapolis valley seeking fertile farms, while fishermen from Cape Cod, searching for land nearer the Grand Banks, settled along the south shore. These New Englanders were accustomed to the dangers and hardships of pioneer life, and as the voyage was short from their old homes they brought most of their farming equipment and household goods with them.

The farmers settled in two townships near Annapolis Royal, at Granville on the north of the Basin and at Annapolis on the south; at Cornwallis (now Kentville), at Horton (now Wolfville), and at Falmouth and Newport in the old Acadian district of Minas and Piziquid. These were inhabited largely by families from Connecticut, Massachusetts and Rhode Island. The great marshes of Chignecto were divided into the three townships of Amherst, Cumberland and Sackville, where many of the first settlers had served in the garrison of Fort Cumberland.

From the Acadian district of Cobequid were created three townships, called Truro, Onslow and Londonderry, which developed into Colchester County. These townships were settled chiefly by Scotch-Irish, either from New Hampshire or directly from Ulster. The principal place in Colchester County was Truro, which in 1823 was described as "a pretty little village." It was surrounded by rich farms selling produce to Halifax and Saint John. There was no hint yet of the flourishing hub of transportation Truro was to become after the building of the railway. The farmers of Colchester County were inclined to be self-sufficient about furniture, or to have it made by local carpenters or carriagemakers. James Waddell (1764-1851) was a cabinetmaker in Truro in the early nineteenth century. He emigrated about 1813 to Halifax from Glasgow, Scotland, and later moved to Rawdon, and then to Truro where his brother, the Rev. John Waddell, was Presbyterian minister. Finally James Waddell settled in South Maitland where he worked as a ship's carpenter. In 1838 Ebenezer Beattie was a cabinetmaker in Londonderry, while Robert Brown, Henry Clark and Edmund Sullivan were cabinetmakers in Truro in 1864.

The government of Nova Scotia paid the expenses of transporting the New Englanders to their new homes, and each family was allowed two tons of cargo. Cattle and other stock, tools and equipment, frames and boards for houses, furniture and household furnishings formed part of the cargo. William and Susannah Haliburton, for instance, brought with them provisions for eighteen months, tents, furniture, spinning wheels, a loom and a few farming implements.

The furniture brought from New England was made of pine, oak, cherry, cedar and black walnut in the prevailing styles. Dr. A. W. H. Eaton has noted in his *History of Kings County* that the planters brought with them from Connecticut black-painted rush-bottom chairs with two, three, four or five slats, tables with drop leaves, high-posted bedsteads, chests of drawers, brass dog's head andirons, bellows, iron shovels and tongs, warming pans, foot stoves, kettles, wool and flax spinning wheels, and a few tall clocks.

For the first few weeks after they arrived the settlers must have lived in tents, while the frames and boards brought from Connecticut, Massachusetts and Rhode Island were quickly erected into houses. Logs were used for foundations and corner posts of some dwellings, the outside being clapboarded with the planks from New England.

The New England farmers and fishermen were self-sufficient craftsmen who could make most of the equipment needed for farming and fishing.

No. 7. Maple arm and side chairs and chest of bird's-eye maple made by James Waddell (1764-1851) in Truro, and now belonging to Mrs. W. P. Grant of Pine Hill, Halifax, a great-grandniece of James Waddell.

They brought with them broad axe and saw, hatchet and jack plane, and used them with confidence and skill in building shelter and knocking up plain tables and chairs and beds.

### FISHERMEN FROM CAPE COD

For years the fishermen of New England had been taking catches off the coast of Nova Scotia, but after the capture of Quebec some of them came to make permanent homes closer to the fishing grounds at such places as Chester, Liverpool, Barrington, Argyle and Yarmouth.

The Cape Cod fishermen moved their families in their own vessels and could therefore bring whatever they liked. The hold would be stowed with provisions, furniture and household goods, and on deck would be the fishermen's boats and implements, boards, any gear that would not suffer from the spray, and sheep and cattle. Some brought frames of buildings taken down to be transported to new sites. In Liverpool the house of Captain Silvanus Cobb was built of material brought from Plymouth in New England.

The Reverend Edwin Crowell has described in *A History of Barrington Township and Vicinity* how Edmund Doane brought his pre-fabricated house to Nova Scotia in 1761. When he decided to emigrate from Massachusetts, he had his two-storey house taken down, the posts cut shorter to make it one storey, and the roof converted into something like a mansard roof. The materials were loaded on a hired vessel, together with a quantity of grain and vegetables, some cows and heifers, a mare, some pigs, and furniture.

Before the Doanes could leave Cape Cod, the vessel was wrecked. Edmund Doane salvaged what he could, hired another ship, and sailed for Nova Scotia. On the way another gale drove the vessel past Barrington to Liverpool. As winter was approaching, the Doanes decided to remain there. Their most valuable possessions were unloaded into a small boat, and at the last minute an old sow was also placed in it. The boat was upset by the sow's restlessness, and all the cargo was lost. Gathering up what they could, they lived for the winter in a fish shed. About the first of June the Doane family again embarked for Barrington, where they arrived safely. Of their livestock, only the old mare was alive, the rest having died from starvation or exposure.

Some idea of the furniture and other property brought to Nova Scotia by the New England fishermen may be obtained from a study of the Liverpool Probate Records. In 1770 the inventory of the estate of James Bunker included:

| | |
|---|---:|
| To a Dwelling house, | £22. 4. 3 |
| To ½ doz. Chair, 6/6. Great Chair, 2/6 | 9. |
| To 1 Round table, 3/4. a Looking Glass, 1/4 | 4. 8 |
| To 1 Square table, 1/4. an old case, /8 warming pan 6/5 | 8. 5 |
| To ½ doz. puter plates, 6/ Iron Bason, /8 | 6. 8 |
| To 1 puter platter, 1/9 do., 2/6. puter Bason, 1/4 | 5. 7 |
| 1 puter Bason, 1/. two wooden Dishes, /7 | 1. 7 |
| 1 milk pigging, /7 Funnel, /7 Earthen Jug, 1 | 1. 5 |
| 2 Iron Skillets, /4, tea Kittle, 1/8. ten Earthen plates, 2/6 | 4. 6 |
| 1 Bed, & beadstead, 24/6. 5 small Knives, 1/1 | 1. 5. 7 |
| 1 Silver Spoon, /5 pair and Irons, 5/ | 10. |
| 1 pot, 2/6. Skillet, 1/8, pr. tongs & skewer 2/ | 6. 2 |
| 1 Box Iron, /8, Spinning wheel, 1/4, foot wheel, 4/6 | 6. 6 |
| 1 meat bag, /4. Iron Crane, 5/ tramil 2/ | 7. 4 |
| 1 Draw knife, 1/2, Scve, /3 Coopers Compass & bit /9 | 2. 2 |
| 1 Quarter of Small Schooner, & appurtenances, | 1. 2. 3 |
| 1 plow Share, & Colter, 10/ old Iron, 1/ Cart wheels, 11/1 | 1. 2. 1 |
| 1 hand Saw, 2/9. old Chair, 2/6 | 5. 3 |
| 3 Cows, 60/ pr cow. half share Land 20£ one sheep 20/ | 29.10. |
| | £59. 3. 3 |

The trees and rocks encouraged lumbering and fishing along the south shore, particularly in Queens County. By 1800 Liverpool was a lively bustling place with spacious houses and prosperous merchants who exported fish and lumber to the West Indies and timber to Britain. In 1838 the population had reached 4,000. There are few cabinetmakers listed in the early days of Queens County, but the flourishing trade made it possible to import furniture from New England, England or Halifax.

Barrington's population increased steadily in the economy based on fishing, shipbuilding and the West Indies trade. Andrew Homer was a cabinetmaker there in 1838.

Ships played a great part in the development of Yarmouth County, which was largely settled by New Englanders. After the War of 1812 shipbuilding became more important, and by 1849 Yarmouth was one of the chief commercial centres of Nova Scotia. In the nineteenth century its citizens had ample opportunities to import furniture and household goods from any part of the world, and also to support such local cabinetmakers as the Huestis and Moulton families and Calvin Wyman and Son.

Windsor not only rivalled Yarmouth in shipbuilding but became a notable cultural centre. Many Nova Scotian Councillors and Halifax merchants had large estates there. Fort Edward had a military garrison, and for many years after its foundation there in 1789 King's was the only college in the province. Penderman Allison was a cabinetmaker in Windsor in the 1790's and John Malcolm a clockmaker.

### THE LOYALISTS

Another group to have a profound influence on Nova Scotian history were the Loyalists. These were people in the thirteen colonies along the Atlantic coast who left their homes because of the Revolution and moved into territories where they could continue to live under the British flag. Among them were government officials, important businessmen, large landowners and leading professional men. By far the greater number, however, were ordinary men without wealth or influence — farmers, tradesmen, apprentices, clergymen, doctors, lawyers, teachers and soldiers. They came by sea from New England, New York, New Jersey, Pennsylvania and the Carolinas. Beginning in the spring of 1783 thousands moved to Canada and to Nova Scotia.

About twenty thousand Loyalists settled in Nova Scotia, doubling the population in one year. Another twelve thousand moved to lands north of the Bay of Fundy, where the new province of New Brunswick was created. In Nova Scotia, Loyalist settlements sprang up along the coast at Digby, Shelburne, Ship Harbour, Sheet Harbour, Sherbrooke, Country Harbour and Guysborough, at Antigonish, and in Cumberland County at Wallace, Pugwash, Westchester, Wentworth and Parrsborough. Loyalist wealth probably accounted for Peter Ball being a cabinetmaker in Guysborough in 1792. Less than a thousand settled in Cape Breton, chiefly at Sydney and Baddeck.

The Loyalists found no rich marshes and cleared fields as had the New Englanders and Scotch-Irish when they arrived. The forest had to be cut down before they could build their homes, and often the land they cleared was rocky and sterile. Few were accustomed to the hard life of the pioneer, for the majority had come from towns or villages where the outlying fields had been claimed from the forest for several generations.

The largest Loyalist town in Nova Scotia was Shelburne, where close to 10,000 people were quartered during the winter of 1783-1784 in frame houses, log huts, shanties, tents and vessels moored in the cove. Only a handful of poor fishermen lived at Port Roseway harbour when the spring fleet of five thousand Loyalists arrived in May 1783, and there was not enough cleared land to pitch a military tent. Benjamin Marston, one of the surveyors sent by the government, noted in his diary that Captain McLean gave him a green turtle weighing seven pounds. "He is to have a house lot, but this must not blind my eyes. He must run the same chance as his neighbours who have no turtle to send." The first house lots were drawn for on May 23, 1783, and by the first of February 1,127 houses had been built.

Naturally, the supply of workmen and materials was not equal to the demand of building a city for 10,000 overnight, although a number of carpenters with tools had come from New York with the spring fleet. In the years 1783 to 1785 the Loyalists spent £500,000 of their private fortunes in Shelburne. The lumber trade flourished, ships were built and sent to engage in the South American whaling trade, and Shelburne developed considerable commerce.

The first settlers to come to Shelburne had arranged their own transportation, and they saw to it that whatever household goods remaining in their possession were transported to Nova Scotia. But the majority of the Loyalists had been driven from their homes to take shelter in New York or Charlestown, and had been forced to leave behind many cherished objects. Perhaps not as much beautiful furniture was brought into the province as we imagine, and little has been found that can be proven to have come to Nova Scotia with a Loyalist family.

The *Royal American Gazette,* one of Shelburne's three newspapers, advertised on June 13, 1785, that Reilly and Braine in Charlotte-lane had just imported a few sets of elegant Windsor chairs of various patterns. Eight-day repeating clocks with mahogany cases were being sold on board the brigantine *Industry,* and mahogany tables, chairs and bedsteads were being auctioned at the Merchants' Coffee House.

For three years each man, woman and child received daily rations of pork and flour supplied by the British government. When these free rations ended the population began to decline. Of the 710 ratepayers in Shelburne in 1786, only 125 appeared on the list of 1796. The surrounding land was rocky, and the fishery could not support a large city. More and more people left, and by the end of the century Shelburne was almost a deserted city. The poorer classes sold their property for a trifle, while the richer continued to hold theirs and took it to another home. Lynde Walter wrote on July 17, 1792, to his brother William, who had requested him to purchase at the auction sales a certain kind of musket: "the sales at auction are nearly done and everybody is ready to leave." On August 30, 1792, he wrote to John Marshall of New York: "You would have had a further quantity [of furniture] by the *Edward,* but she is full of goods appertaining to the different passengers."

Some of the Loyalists who had founded Shelburne returned to the United States. Others went to the West Indies, New Brunswick, Prince Edward Island and Ontario, and to Halifax and to other towns in Nova Scotia already established by the New Englanders, where they could practise their trades or professions. Many houses were taken down and removed to Liverpool, Barrington, Halifax and Saint John. Others were used as fuel.

After 1787 there were many auctions of possessions of those forced to leave Shelburne. Land was sold for practically nothing, but furniture brought a fair price because speculators could ship it away. On June 21, 1787, five Windsor chairs belonging to John Sergeant were sold for 25 shillings, a square table for 5 shillings, a bedstead and curtains for 40 shillings, and a pair of candlesticks for 7/6. In May 1788 Peter Bogle, one of the leading Shelburne merchants, purchased the following from Bartholomew Bower: a dozen Windsor chairs for 60 shillings, two arm chairs with cushions for 15 shillings, a mahogany table for 40 shillings, a kitchen table for 9 shillings and a pine table for half a crown, a bedstead and curtains for 100 shillings, a dressing glass for 25 shillings and a large looking glass for 30 shillings, two carpets for 80 shillings, two large pictures for 40 shillings, a dutch oven for 12/6, three iron pots for 4/6, and a frying pan for half a crown. About the same time a lot, house, brewhouse and other buildings on Brewer's Lane were sold for £9.

The Loyalist immigration brought to Nova Scotia many educated men who appreciated schools, colleges, newspapers and the amenities of culture, and who were willing to strive for these in their new homes. Nonetheless, the highly skilled craftsmen, such as goldsmiths, watchmakers and cabinet-makers, found it difficult to earn a living in the new settlements. Four cabinet-makers are listed in the assessment roll for the county of Shelburne for the year 1786: William Black, and Daniel, Henry and Job Goddard. In 1787 William Black and John Spiers were the only cabinetmakers. The Goddards had moved from Water Street to Fanning Lane, but were listed as carpenters. They remained on Fanning Lane until September 1788, when they probably removed to Halifax. The prosperity caused by the American Revolution and the coming of the Loyalists had increased the population of Halifax to 5,000. There in the capital were merchants, officials and military men who could afford to patronize skilled cabinetmakers such as the Goddards. No examples of their work have yet been found at Shelburne or Halifax.

Daniel, Job and Henry Goddard received free land grants in Shelburne in 1784 as part compensation for their loyalty to the Crown. John, Lemuel, senior, and Lemuel, junior, and Elias Kingston Goddard also received land grants in Shelburne County.

These men were related to the famous John Goddard of Newport, Rhode Island. Mr. Herbert O. Brigham, librarian of the Rhode Island Historical Society, has stated: "John Goddard, a famous Newport cabinetmaker, had a brother Daniel Goddard, who 'went off with the enemy on October 25th, 1779.' We have no record of a Job Goddard but Job was a very common Townsend name and John Goddard married Job Townsend's daughter. I would assume that the Job may well have been from the Newport Goddard family." John and Hannah (Townsend) Goddard had sons named Daniel, John, Job and Henry among a family of thirteen, and they may have been the Shelburne grantees, according to a descendant. Daniel Goddard of Digby, a cabinetmaker, sold his Shelburne town lots in 1819. Some of the Loyalist

Goddards lived in New Brunswick where a young girl remembered her grandfather, dressed in old-fashioned knee breeches and with lace at the cuffs of his coat, crying at their poverty. This branch of the family were outstanding carpenters, who were always called upon whenever a building had to be roofed.

John Goddard of Newport, Rhode Island, is celebrated for his mahogany block front secretary-desks, which are highly prized by collectors. They are characterized by the shell-carving on the front of the writing-leaf, on the doors of the bookcase compartments above, and on the pigeon-hole drawers of the interior, and also by a fondness for the broken-pediment top with flame finials.

### THE COMING OF THE SCOTS

The eastern part of the peninsula of Nova Scotia and Cape Breton Island have been settled and influenced by the Scots, who were driven from their homes by the industrial revolution and by their landlords' discovery that raising sheep was more profitable than maintaining small tenant farmers. The vanguard of the Highland migration arrived in September 1773 at Pictou, where they found a land covered with primeval forest.

When the Rev. James MacGregor, a Presbyterian missionary, arrived in Pictou in 1786, he found that Squire Robert Patterson had the only frame house in Pictou. The Rev. George Patterson has described in *The Memoir of Rev. James MacGregor, D.D.,* how the majority of the Scots lived in log huts with moss stuffed in the chinks and with roofs formed of the bark of trees. "Their furniture was of the rudest description, frequently a block of wood or a rude bench, made out a slab, in which four sticks had been inserted as legs, served for chair or table. Their food was commonly served up in wooden dishes or in wooden plates, and eaten with wooden spoons. . . . Money was scarcely seen, and almost all trade was done by barter; wheat and maple sugar, being the principal circulating medium."

Soldiers from Highland regiments were disbanded in Pictou County after the American Revolution, and more Scottish families continued to arrive, particularly after the Napoleonic wars ended in 1815. Presbyterians tended to settle in Pictou County, Roman Catholics in Antigonish County.

The timber that covered the country from the edge of the sea to the summits of the hills proved one of the most valuable resources of the inhabitants. The timber trade with Britain increased steadily from 1774, and after the closing of the Baltic by Napoleon's continental blockade against British commerce the price rose to an unprecedented height. In 1803 about fifty vessels were loaded at Pictou with timber for Great Britain, and from 1800 to 1820 it was calculated that exports from the port averaged £100,000 per annum. Products of the General Mining Association from the Albion Mines (now Stellarton) were shipped from the port, for Pictou was the only port of entry for the north shore. It was a landing place for immigrants, a centre of commerce and shipbuilding, and an educational centre with its Pictou Academy. By 1830 it was the most populous locality in the province outside of Halifax, and rivalled Halifax both in population and in intellectual activity. This prosperity and the flourishing trade of the port help to explain why Pictou has had more cabinetmakers than any other part of the province except the Halifax area.

Although there were some French and Loyalists living in Cape Breton, the island could not be said to be settled until the waves of Scottish immigrants arrived in the early decades of the nineteenth century. Over twenty-five thousand Scots landed in Cape Breton from 1815 to 1851. By 1838 Cape Breton had a population of 40,000. At Sydney, where the Loyalists had again demonstrated their inability to raise a city in the wilderness, less than 500 people lived. Arichat was the most important and thriving town in Cape Breton, largely because it was the headquarters of the Jersey merchants and fishermen. Not a single cabinetmaker has been found on the old census records, probably because Cape Breton's economy was a pioneer one dependent on farming and fishing until the development of the coal mines and the steel mills in the twentieth century.

### THE GOLDEN AGE

In the second and third decades of the nineteenth century Nova Scotians experienced an intellectual awakening that was to have a far-reaching influence on their political, economic, social and cultural life. Although there had been a large immigration after the Napoleonic wars, the majority of the 200,000 people living in Nova Scotia in 1838 had been born and bred in the province, which had now advanced beyond the pioneering stage when every effort had to be concentrated on earning a living. This progress is reflected in the increasing number of cabinetmakers in Nova Scotia. The rise of local patriotism for the province of their birth became a natural development, and the winning of responsible government in 1848 freed Nova Scotians politically.

An increasing prosperity based on an economy of wood, wind and sail, a wider knowledge of the world and an awareness of their intellectual powers had given Nova Scotians confidence in themselves and their destiny. This golden age lasted until the abrogation of the Reciprocity Treaty with the United States in April 1866, and the gradual replacement of wooden ships by iron and steel brought an end to the great age of Bluenose shipbuilding. The number of cabinetmakers and furniture makers in Nova Scotia reached its peak in the 1860's, before succumbing to competition from furniture factories in central Canada and the United States.

My researches have uncovered the names of many cabinetmakers who have worked in Nova Scotia, but the full history of cabinet making in the Maritime Provinces has yet to be written. It is hoped that readers will examine carefully the lists in the appendices so that they may be able to identify articles that could add to the knowledge of future collectors. One of the outstanding cabinetmakers of New Brunswick in the nineteenth century was John Warren Moore (1812-1893), the grandson of a Loyalist. After his marriage in 1833 he moved to St. Stephen, where he became noted for the thorough workmanship and finish of his furniture. Surviving examples include beds, bureaus and mirrors, chairs, sewing tables, music tables, a nine foot dining-table of solid mahogany, writing desks and china cabinets; over thirty of them have been collected in the home of his great-granddaughter in Toronto.

In silver and ceramics, glass and furniture, the products of the studios of the Maritime Provinces will, when properly and fully recorded, fill out the story of the cultural and aesthetic development of Canada. Each art, however, requires a book to itself. In this volume I have attempted to chronicle the history of Nova Scotian furniture and of some of the men who created it.

# CHAPTER TWO

# Cabinetmakers and Their Woods

Both in England and in France a sharp distinction was drawn among carpenters, joiners, cabinetmakers and wood carvers. The carpenter was the one who drove the nails while the joiner fastened joints with mortise and tenon. The English joiners of the seventeenth century had many disputes with both carpenters and shipwrights in order to form a separate guild.

By 1725 the joiners who made the highboy and the slope front desk had started calling themselves cabinetmakers. In Europe this was followed by a further distinction between cabinetmaker and chairmaker. The cabinetmaker was a "case furnituremaker," a case being defined as "any receptacle, cabinet or box used for holding things." A chair represented the labour of a wood carver, whose work was fitted together by a joiner.

In America these crafts were not so carefully distinguished. Cabinetmakers made all types of furniture, although some craftsmen specialized in the manufacture of chairs. Now it is customary to group all furniture craftsmen working in wood as cabinetmakers. The craft of cabinetmaking required not only technical skill but considerable education, at least a knowledge of plane geometry and an ability to read pattern books.

In the days of the pioneers a handyman or carpenter would build everyday furniture, or a farmer would take time in the winter to construct tables or chairs or a chest for his sweetheart or wife, or a shipwright temporarily unemployed might make furniture for a local merchant. Descendants who have inherited furniture of this type proudly point out that it has been produced in Nova Scotia. In my list of cabinetmakers in Appendix A, however, I have included only those who are listed as cabinetmakers in a census or directory, or who advertised in the newspapers as such. Undoubtedly many of those listed as carpenters, shipwrights, turners or carriagemakers also produced furniture. For instance, Elisha Cahoon, James and Joseph Atkins, and George Reinhardt of Port Medway in Queens County are remembered as furniture makers. In McAlpine's *Nova Scotia Directory* for 1868-69 Charles, Joseph, James, Samuel and Thomas Atkins, Foster Cahoon, and Augustus Foster are listed as carpenters living at Port Medway. Enoch Dodge, coachmaker in Granville township in 1838, made various pieces of furniture, and is occasionally confused with Edwin Dodge, cabinetmaker at Digby.

Some form of apprenticeship was practised in Nova Scotia, for the *Colonial Patriot* in 1829 carried a notice from Samuel Paulan, cabinetmaker, stating that his indented apprentice, fifteen-year-old William Fraser, had absconded, and offering a reward for his return. In the same year two boys, sixteen and fourteen years old, were asking "to be apprenticed to the Cabinet Making Trade in Halifax."

In August 1832 John Baxter, a cabinetmaker of Halifax, was advertising that John Gordon, one of his carpenters, had broken open a drawer and stolen seven pounds in bank notes and some counters which he had passed off for gold coin on Mr. Troup, watchmaker of Halifax. Gordon had been arrested, but had managed to escape from two constables.

The Age of Oak, the Age of Walnut, and the Age of Mahogany, which are so important in the study of English furniture, do not occur in Nova Scotia. Some idea of the native woods used by craftsmen in the Maritimes may be obtained from the analysis of native trees and their products by Dr. Abraham Gesner, the discoverer of kerosene, in his book *The Industrial Resources of Nova Scotia,* which was published in 1849.

### PINE

Dr. Gesner remarked that white pine was the most valuable product of the forests of British America, and that he had seen white pine trees 200 feet high with a trunk five feet in diameter. Indeed, the Highlanders who came

No. 8. Pine cupboards. *Left:* "The Ten Mile House," Bedford, N.S. 1960. *Right:*
Provincial Museum, Citadel Hill, Halifax, N.S. PHOTO BY E. LONGARD.

to Pictou in 1773 refused to settle in the forests because of the difficulty of
clearing the gigantic pine and oak trees and the fear of being lost in the dense
undergrowth, where Indians and wild beasts might be lurking.

White pine wood was universally employed because it was easily worked
and had a straight, light grain. Judge M. B. DesBrisay said in his *History of
Lunenburg County* that the pine sills of an old house built in Lunenburg in
1757 were still in good condition in 1890, and that about 1845 a table-top

twenty-six inches across had been made from one pine board cut from a tree near Bridgewater. The sort of tree that could be squared off and cut into such surfaces has disappeared through export and fire.

No. 9. Pine chests. The pine blanket chest at top left came from Mount Denson in Hants County, the one at upper right from Queens County. Both show Empire influence, and are at the Provincial Museum, Citadel Hill, Halifax. The miniature pine chest, 28″ by 13″, at bottom left, is from the collection of Dr. C. M. Jones, Halifax, as is the child's pine chest at bottom right.

No. 10. Nova Scotian pine dressing table in the collection of H. E. Dawes, Ottawa, Ontario.

Because it was plentiful, cheap, and easy to work, pine has probably been used more extensively than any other kind of wood for the simpler kinds of household furniture. The New Englanders who came to Nova Scotia were accustomed to making things of pine — knife boxes, benches, stools, settles,

No. 11. Nova Scotian pine secretary-bookcase in the collection of H. E. Dawes, Ottawa, Ontario.

tables, blanket chests, chests of drawers, highboys, candle stands, desks, cupboards and spoon racks. The bottoms and sides of drawers of mahogany or walnut desks and bureaus were often made of pine, and a mahogany veneer was frequently applied to a pine carcass. Pine furniture made in Nova Scotia

No. 12. Pine courting mirror in Grand Pré Museum, Grand Pré, N.S. PHOTO BY
W. WOOD.

was without any great amount of ornamentation except for mouldings and a few turnings that presented a plain, compact and neat unit.

What was the finish used on pine furniture? Much of the early work, without doubt, was scrubbed clean, giving the wood the beautiful soft texture it naturally acquires. Other pieces were coloured with a dull red pigment mixed with skim milk; this sank far into the grain of the wood and became quite permanent. Pine has a cream colour when new, but when old it is brownish yellow and may turn the most astonishing shades under the action of time and light.

MAPLE AND BIRCH

In the eighteenth century maple and birch grew in the forests of Nova Scotia, often occurring in fancy grains, and they were widely used. Dr. Gesner explains that the seasoned wood of the sugar or rock maple was of a light chocolate colour, heavy, close in texture and strong, and that the wood was "extensively employed by cabinetmakers for furniture" in Nova Scotia.

The woody fibres of the maple tree were often accidentally twisted, curled or dotted to create the "curly maple" or "bird's-eye maple", in the same way as the accidental arrangement of the wood produces the "burl" wood of walnut

No. 13. Table of curly or "tiger" maple with turned legs and two drop leaves. Many examples of this type may be found in Nova Scotia. The Provincial Museum, Citadel Hill, Halifax. PHOTO BY E. LONGARD.

No. 14. Schoolmaster's desk made of maple and birch in Pictou County.   In possession of S. MacLaren, Pictou, N.S. PHOTO BY E. LONGARD.

or the "crotch" wood of mahogany. "Curly maple" comes from a twisting of the grain of any one of several varieties, particularly the sugar maple. The "bird's-eye" figure is formed by little spots supposed to resemble birds' eyes, and is found in the sugar maple only.

Maple and birch appear to have been the sophisticated native woods used in Nova Scotia. Not so fine as walnut or mahogany, and not so common as pine, maple was intended for the living room or the bedrooms, not for the formal "parlour." Many beautiful "curly" maple tables and chests of drawers were made showing the Sheraton influence. Other chests of drawers have fronts of "bird's-eye" maple.

No. 15. Miniature maple chest, 25″ by 22″ by 11″, made in Halifax County. From the collection of Dr. C. M. Jones, Halifax, N.S. PHOTO BY WILLIAM WOOD.

Being an extremely hard wood, maple was seldom used for carving. A particularly fine example, however, is the despatch box presented by Mayor James Duggan on behalf of the corporation and citizens of Halifax on May 2, 1873, to Lieutenant-Governor Sir Hastings Doyle on his retirement from office.

No. 16. Doyle's despatch box. Provincial Museum, Citadel Hill, Halifax, N.S.

The box is beautifully constructed of carved maple-wood, designed and made by James McEwan, a skilful cabinetmaker and carver of Halifax. Its greatest length is 17", greatest width 11.50", and greatest height 11.40". It has four short columns at the corners, foliated panels on the sides, and sprays of may-flowers on the receding sides of the upper section. The casket was originally surmounted by the figure of a moose in Nova Scotian gold and silver, executed by John Herbin, jeweller, historian and poet of Wolfville. It is shown entire in the full-length oil portrait of Doyle by A. R. Venables of London which hangs in the Province House, Halifax. Doyle had the box until his death in 1883, when it passed to his brother, Rt. Hon. John S. Doyle-North, and on his death in 1894 to his son, the 11th Baron North, and was purchased by a

London dealer at the sale of the latter's effects at Wroxton Abbey, Oxfordshire, England, in May, 1933. From this dealer Harry Piers bought it for the Provincial Museum of Science in 1934.

At the International Exhibition at London in 1862, McEwan and Reid of Halifax displayed a drawing-room chair made of maple, cut from a tree on the grounds of Prince's Lodge, the estate of the Duke of Kent, father of Queen Victoria. The front legs and the rail were ornamented with Indian cups, pigeon berries and blossoms, solomon's seal and mayflowers, while the

No. 17. Birch bed from Queens County, turned by a foot lathe. Provincial Museum, Citadel Hill, Halifax, N.S. PHOTO BY E. LONGARD.

back formed a wreath of roses, thistles and shamrocks, crowned by mayflowers —the emblem of Nova Scotia.

According to Dr. Gesner, the sweet-scented wood of the black birch was remarkably close-grained, and "often diversified by reddish and chocolate coloured stripes and spots" similar to mahogany that "have given it a celebrity for tables, bedsteads, and other kinds of furniture." The wood of the canoe or paper birch was white with a red heart, fine gained and light, and therefore used widely by cabinetmakers and wheelwrights. Indians also constructed their canoes and coffins out of this tree's bark, which was also applied as a primitive insulation over crevices between boards before shingling or clapboarding.

### CHERRY

In the United States cherry wood was employed for wheels of wooden clocks, and for beautiful and durable furniture, explains Dr. Gesner, but he does not say that it was common in Nova Scotia, probably because it is scattered through the forests, a clump here and another there. Furniture made of cherry, when finished, took on a rich red-brown colour that was slightly lighter in tone than that of walnut. Dr. A. W. H. Eaton mentions in his *History of Kings County* that the New England planters who came to the Annapolis valley in the 1760's brought with them cherry chests, tables, chairs and cases of drawers.

### WALNUT

The New Englanders may also have brought with them walnut furniture, as large stands of walnut grew in Pennsylvania and Virginia, and the wood was imported into New England seaport towns. Some walnut grew in New England forests, but it was brown rather than red.

Walnut is not native to Nova Scotia, and I have not seen any advertisements of its importation in the early days of our history. The use of oak and walnut was not common in Nova Scotia until late Victorian times, when furniture of these woods was made in the factories of John Reed of Bridgetown, Gordon and Keith of Halifax, and others.

### THE EMINENCE OF MAHOGANY

Prior to the importation of mahogany, cabinetmakers would use local hardwoods and make adaptations of English design. These English designers made some of our finest examples of furniture, blending maple, birch and bird's-eye maple, and this work is today eagerly sought by collectors. By 1790 mahogany was imported into the province, and an era began in which furniture was made of that wood.

Mahogany! What dreams of a glorious past the word inspires! Before our vision comes, first, the stalwart Sir Walter Raleigh, beating his stormy way across trackless oceans to the far shores of a strange land, that he might gather treasures and place them at the feet of his queen. Among the treasures were planks of mahogany to be wrought into exquisite furniture.

After him comes Thomas Chippendale the elder, who so loved this "royal wood" that he wrote: "My Mahogany ribband chairs which, if I may speak without vanity, are the best I have ever seen or perhaps ever made." George Hepplewhite and others produced mahogany masterpieces that, while somewhat influenced by Chippendale because of his book *The Gentleman and Cabinet Maker's Director* (first published in 1754), nevertheless expressed the maker's individuality and character.

Then comes Thomas Sheraton, almost the last of the great English masters, who published *The Cabinetmaker and Upholsterer's Drawing Book* in 1791, and who said: "Other woods formerly used for Cabinet-Work are quite Laid by since the introduction of Mahogany."

There are several legends about the introduction of mahogany into England. On one of his cruises Sir Walter Raleigh was forced to stop at an island in the West Indies to make repairs to his ship, and was given mahogany by the natives. After he returned to England in 1595, Queen Elizabeth visited the vessel and admired the fine colour of the planks in the deck. Sir Walter used some of the wood in making a table for Her Majesty, but oak and walnut remained the popular woods.

About 1724 a sea captain brought some mahogany planks to England to be used in building his brother's house. The wood proved to be too hard for

No. 18. Chippendale style mahogany chair at the Quinlan House, Mahone Bay, Lunenburg County. PHOTO BY E. G. L. WETMORE.

the carpenters to cut, however, so it was sold to a cabinetmaker who constructed a bureau from it. The Duchess of Buckingham admired this piece and ordered one made out of the same wood.

At this time an unsually severe winter on the Continent had caused a walnut tree famine, and London cabinetmakers were unable to import from France all the walnut they needed. In this crisis mahogany was imported in large quantities from San Domingo and Cuba. Soon English cabinetmakers learned that mahogany was a beautiful wood, and that its texture made it ideal for delicate carving.

In the United States mahogany was extensively used for furniture from 1730 to 1840. A few pieces had been made before that date, and mahogany furniture was listed in an inventory in Philadelphia in 1708.

The Rev. George Hill in his *Memoir of Sir Brenton Halliburton* described the furniture in the wealthier homes in Halifax about 1800:

It was usually made of a mahogany wood, of a rich, dark color; the dining-room table was plain, but massive, supported by heavy legs, often ornamented at the feet with the carved resemblance of a lion's claw; the side-board was high, rather narrow and inelegant; the secretary, or covered writing desk, was bound with numberless brass plates at the edges. . . the chairs cumbrous, straight-backed, with their cushions covered with black horse-hair cloth. . . the great arm-chair deserved its title, for it was wide and deep enough to contain not only the master of the household, but, if he pleased, several of his children beside. . . . The bedsteads were those still known as four-posted, invariably curtained, and with a canopy overhead. . . . The chests of drawers and the ladies' wardrobes were covered with the ubiquitous brazen plates, and being kept bright, gave the room an air of comfort and cleanliness. . . it was not an unfounded complaint. . . that the time of one servant was wholly engrossed with the daily routine of burnishing the metal on the furniture and doors, and polishing the wood.

In the country districts of Nova Scotia mahogany furniture was scarce until the nineteenth century, although it is likely that as soon as mahogany became common in Boston it appeared in Halifax, and some was imported from England. Dr. A. W. H. Eaton was of the opinion that little mahogany

No. 19. Mahogany mirror imported from England by A. De La Torre, a merchant
of Halifax, in 1828. In the collection of H. E. Dawes, Ottawa, Ontario.
PHOTO BY E. DAWES.

furniture was to be found in Kings County until 1840. In 1816 a mahogany desk valued at £5 and two small mahogany desks at £2 were listed in the inventory of the estate of the Rev. Thomas Shreve of Lunenburg.

*My minor is identical to this except for an additional curve in centre front A*

No. 20. Mahogany swinging mirror made by W. E. Heffernan of Halifax in 1870, and now in the possession of the author. PHOTO BY E. LONGARD.

The mahogany used in Nova Scotia came chiefly from the Caribbean Islands, principally Cuba and San Domingo. Beginning before the American Revolution, ships from Nova Scotia carried fish and lumber to the West Indies, and brought back rum, molasses, brown sugar, salt and occasionally mahogany. In 1786 four thousand feet of mahogany were auctioned at Shelburne, and in 1807 a prize brig loaded with mahogany arrived at Halifax. Mahogany logs were imported into Halifax in 1816, and cabinetmakers protested to the

No. 21. Drum table made by Tulles, Pallister and M'Donald of Halifax. This rare
Sheraton mahogany library table has a revolving top on reeded pillar, with
original handles. It is 2′ 10″ in diameter and 2′ 5″ high.   PHOTO BY
COURTESY OF MR. IAN C. MORGAN, MONTREAL, P.Q.

Legislature in 1826 that mahogany could be purchased in New York or Boston
for half the asking price at Halifax.

At the time of his death in 1804 Lieutenant-Colonel James Delancey of
Round Hill in Annapolis County, who had come to Nova Scotia as a Loyalist
from New York, had one pair of mahogany dining tables valued at £5.10,

another valued at £1.14.6, while a small mahogany table sold for 10 shillings, and six old mahogany chairs for £2.14.0. Two eight-day clocks in mahogany cases and a mahogany bedstead were auctioned at Halifax by Bowie and DeBlois in May 1818.

One of the finest pieces of mahogany furniture produced in Nova Scotia was made in 1810 by Tulles, Pallister and M'Donald, cabinetmakers and upholsterers on Barrington Street in Halifax. This Sheraton mahogany drum table, with revolving top on a reeded pillar, was for sale in London, England, in 1956, and was identified as Nova Scotian by two trade labels in the drawers.

It was described as follows:

I am enclosing 2 photographs of the most attractive and high quality circular library or drum table of which the very great interest is the 2 trade labels which are in 2 of the drawers and I have in fact neither heard of nor seen any piece of Canadian furniture with original trade labels.

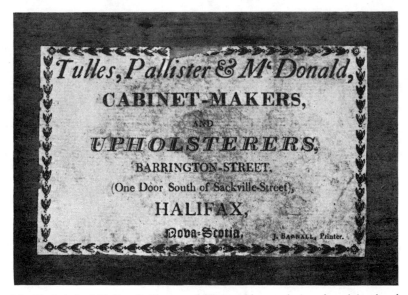

No. 22. Label of Tulles, Pallister and M'Donald, actual size, found in the drawer of the Drum Table, 1810. PHOTO BY COURTESY OF MR. IAN C. MORGAN, MONTREAL, P.Q.

The table itself is veneered with very finely figured mahogany including the top and it has a tripod pedestal of extremely nice design with chased castors. The only thing that is in any way not original is that it has lost its original block on top of the stem on which the table originally revolved and this has been replaced by a bearer of oak. This is a thing that so often happens to this type of table as it is on the block that most of the wear occurs and when a table has become wobbly it is unfortunate that so often the block gets replaced instead of being repaired but I consider that there can be no question whatever that the stand is original to the top.

There are in the frieze 4 square drawers and the intervening spaces are of course dummy. Linings of the drawers are of pine. . . .

I would like to say that so far as I can tell there is nothing in the construction of the table that would lead one to think it was otherwise but English if it were not for the trade labels in the drawers but on the other hand I think with these labels the inference must be that the table was made in Canada probably by craftsmen who went over. One would not expect a trade label of this kind in a table unless it was made by the people named thereon.

### EARLY CABINETMAKERS' MARKS

Tulles, Pallister and M'Donald advertised in the *Nova Scotia Royal Gazette* of June 18, 1810, that they "still continue to carry on the above business in all its various branches, in Barrington-street, one door south of Sackville-street, where all orders will be punctually attended to." They had a large supply of first quality mahogany, and were offering mahogany logs or boards for sale. This advertisement was still running in September 1811.

Shortly afterwards the partnership must have been dissolved, for in February 1812 Thomas Pallister, cabinetmaker, was doing business "in *Hollis Street,* nearly opposite Mr. Merrick's, where all orders in his line, will be thankfully received, and executed with neatness and dispatch." In October of that year, John Tulles had removed to the house "lately occupied by *Mrs. Gracie,* and nearly opposite the Ordnance Gate."

Very few furniture makers identified their work either by labelling or stamping, because in England chairmakers and cabinetmakers were not obliged to mark their products. Labels with name and address of craftsmen were printed on sheets of paper, cut by scissors (like the early unperforated

No. 23. Mahogany secretary-bookcase made by A. Morton, Halifax, N.S., about 1826. From the collection of Miss E. C. Monk, Montreal, P.Q.

stamps), and pasted on the furniture in an inconspicuous place such as a drawer. The scarcity of labelled furniture is partly due to the labels having been worn away by the rubbing of articles placed in the drawers, or by being deliberately scraped off by owners who thought them ugly.

Trade cards were also fastened to pieces of furniture. These were intended for advertising and were handed to prospective customers. They are often highly decorative and contain illustrations of various types of furniture, the sign of the craftsman's shop, and other details. On page 73 may be seen an illustration of James Gordon's trade card which was handed to Dr. T. B. Akins, first Archivist of Nova Scotia, at the Nova Scotia Exhibition of 1854 with a notation on the back "Walnut Chairs for Sale. Price £2. 10.0."

In the seventeenth century branded initials became common on joined chairs and stools, but not so common on tables and chests. In the eighteenth century and after, chairmakers in provincial centres in England continued to brand their chairs. Although a great many chairmakers' branding irons were in use, they are rare today.

At the end of the eighteenth century the stamping (not branding) of the makers' name in full was used instead of a label. The usual place chosen for the stamp was the top edge of the drawer. In the nineteenth century this stamping of the full name was adopted by a number of London firms.

Some unmarked furniture may be identified by the preservation of the original bill of sale. Much of Chippendale's furniture has been identified in this way.

Much furniture made in Nova Scotia is not stamped or labelled and it is impossible to tell whether it was made in the province or imported from Great Britain or the United States. In March 1820, William Gordon of Halifax was advertising for sale in the *Acadian Recorder* the following elegant and fashionable furniture, all manufactured by himself:

"elegant pillar and claw, plain dining, pembroke, card and sofa Tables; ladies' work and toilet do; Secretaries and Book Cases; Chests of Drawers, and Bason Stands; elegant brass ornamented and carved Sideboards; carved, plain, hair covered and common Sofas, and couches; Mahogany and Windsor Chairs; elegant high post Bedsteads, with carved and cable posts, superior to any done in this country before; plain reeded and birch do; single and double field do.; do. with French roofs; ladies' music Stools, and portable Desks."

Mr. Smith "from London, UNDERTAKER, UPHOLSTERER, CABINET AND CHAIR-MAKER" opened a new furniture wareroom at No. 43, Jacobs' Brick Building, Upper Water Street, in Halifax, and offered for sale in December 1821 "elegant Mahogany High Post Bedsteads with Mahogany Cornices. . . Spring and Rocking Cradles, Patent and portable Dining, Sofa, Card, Pembroke, Ladies' Work and Toilet Tables. . . Mahogany Secretaries and Book Cases. . . Hair Cloth, Grecian and common Sofas, and Couches; Mahogany and Birch portable low priced Chests of Drawers, an elegant, convenient piece of Furniture for the army, navy, and travelling gentlemen." He manufactured all sorts of furniture.

Furniture made by such men as William Gordon, Mr. Smith and others is not recognized as Nova Scotian unless it is stamped or labelled. Other pieces may be identified from time to time as they appear at auctions the way the drum table made by Tulles, Pallister and M'Donald has been discovered, making us aware of the variety of beautiful furniture made in this province.

# CHAPTER THREE

# Chairs and Their Makers

Chairs are more important to the furniture collector than any other article because they were made in every style and period and because they are more plentiful and easier to collect, having generally been made in sets.

The French were the first to make chairs in Nova Scotia. Examples in the Fort Beauséjour Museum, near Amherst, show that Acadian chairs had a high sloping back with sturdy square legs cut from wood found in the neighbourhood.

Prior to 1749, and indeed for years after, few chairs were to be found in Nova Scotia. The cargo-carrying capacity of the tiny ships that voyaged to its shores from Europe was limited, and the early settlers could bring with them only necessities. Chairs were not essential for life in the New World. Once arrived at their new home, any handyman or carpenter could make a few benches or stools, or the children could sit on a piece cut from the trunk of a tree.

Among the middle classes in the British Isles and Europe during the seventeenth century, chairs were a luxury; a chair was still considered to be a seat of honour and placed the sitter a little apart from and above the others. The only armed chair would be reserved for the head of the household or his guests; the women and children sat on stools or benches. One old oak table has been found with the end stretcher worn almost flat where the head of the family rested his feet at mealtime while he leaned back in his chair. The other stretchers show no wear because the rest of the family sat upright on benches, with their feet on the floor.

The settlers who came with Cornwallis to found Halifax in 1749 brought few household furnishings. Fifty trades were represented among this group, however, ranging from armourer to wool comber. There should have been little difficulty in setting up new homes, but these English colonists were not accustomed to life in an uncleared forest and had not developed the ability to make do with the materials at hand. They were soon joined by hundreds of New Englanders looking for new opportunities and lured by the prospect of free government spending, and among them would be men able and willing to supply any lack of the English craftsmen.

The five thousand New England farmers and fishermen who came to Nova Scotia in the 1760's had been long established in their old homes and brought with them tools, stock, furniture and food, lumber and sometimes even the frames of their former houses. They brought chairs with them, and because the majority of settlers came from the British Isles the seaboard colonists would have chairs of modified English design.

An inventory of the estate of James Bunker of Barrington in 1770 lists among other furniture one half-dozen chairs at six shillings and sixpence and a great chair valued at half a crown. Thomas West's estate at Barrington in the same year had three red chairs valued at five shillings and four black chairs worth two shillings and eight pence. Included in the share of her late husband's estate given in 1775 to Mrs. Deborah Dogget of Liverpool were "one great Chair, one Great Chair high ditto & Cushion, three Back Chairs."

One of the early cabinetmakers of Queens County was Elijah Minard. He had run away from his home in Connecticut to join the expedition to Louisbourg in 1758, and had fought in New York State and in Cuba before eventually coming to Nova Scotia. There in 1767 he was admitted as one of the proprietors in the township of Liverpool, and also owned land at Port Medway and at Milton.

Elijah Minard is described as a "wheelwright," but it is said that the first Windsor chairs were made by English wheelwrights using the tools and technique of fashioning a wagon wheel. Minard is remembered as a maker of chairs, and at least five of his chairs were treasured by his descendants a century after his death.

One chair carefully preserved by his descendants is made of ash, and is forty-two inches high. The lower part of the front legs is turned in the same manner as the upper part, while the rear legs are plain. It has a banister back, turned finials, and stretchers three spindles wide. The backs of the slats are fancy, the fronts smooth and plain. The seat is the original one of woven rope.

The chairs popular in New England at the time of the migration to Nova Scotia were the slat-back or ladder-back, the banister-back, the corner or round-about chair, and the Windsor chair. These types were made in Nova Scotia for a century.

Curly maple was a favourite material, since its grain was especially decorative for turned parts, back splats and shaped arms. Both slat-back and banister-back were usually painted dull black and had rush seats. In the early days of Halifax, an old man on Hollis Street made rough chairs with rush-bottomed seats. If he happened to be out of rushes, his customers had to wait until the rushes grew, were cut down and dried.

The roundabout or corner chair, which was common in the thirteen colonies both as a simple turned chair and with cabriole legs and ornamental back splats, has not been found in Nova Scotia until the Victorian period.

Traditionally, the Windsor chair received its name from having been discovered by King George I in a cottage near that town. His Majesty is said to have found this chair so comfortable that he ordered some for Windsor Castle. Chairs of this type were popular in English farmhouses and won the approval of generations of innkeepers. Dr. Johnson declared a tavern chair to be the throne of felicity.

In the United States, Philadelphia has the earliest records of Windsor chairs. They were in use there about 1725 and in 1763 a New York newspaper was advertising "Philadelphia-made Windsor chairs." General George Washington had thirty Windsor chairs for his guests on the east portico of Mount Vernon, while President Thomas Jefferson bought four dozen Windsor arm chairs in 1801 for $192.

English Windsor chairs have a solid splat in the centre of the back, with spindles on either side. Windsor chairs were made in the American colonies before the Revolution in several forms: comb-back, spindle-back, fan-back, and the writing Windsor with a large arm. Various woods were used, sometimes hickory for the spindles, birch for legs and spindles, ash or pine for seats.

In the nineteenth century a few touches of the Sheraton style were added to the plain Windsor chair to form the types known as the rod-back and the arrow-back. The straight lines of Sheraton may be seen in the bamboo-turned box stretchers, the squarish seat, and the sloping back with the rod-spindles or three to five arrow-shaped vertical splats that fit into the flat crest rail. Arrow-back Windsors, with and without arms, combpiece and rockers, were popular in the United States from 1810 to 1835. The arrow-back was the only Windsor made in quantity as a rocking chair.

In America the making of Windsor chairs soon became a specialized craft. A considerable number of cabinetmakers produced no other furniture and styled themselves "Windsor chair makers." There was even a further specialization, as Sam Slick describes in *The Clockmaker: Or Sayings and Doings of Samuel Slick of Slickville*:

When I was down to Rhode Island, larnin', bronzin', gildin', and sketchin' for the clock business, I worked at odd times for the Honourable Eli Wad, a foundationalist—a painting for him. A foundationalist, said I; what is that? is it a religious sect? No, said he, it's a bottom maker. He only made bottoms, he didn't make arms and legs, and he sold these wooden bottoms to the chair-makers. He did 'em by a sarcular saw and a turnin' lathe, and he turned 'em off amazin' quick; he made a fortin' out of the invention, for he shipped 'em to every part of the Union. The select men objected to his sign of bottom-maker; they said it didn't sound pretty, and he altered it to foundationalist. That was one cause the speck turned out so well, for everyone that seed it a'most stopt to inquire what it meant, and it brought his patent into great vogue; many's the larf folks had over that sign, I tell you.

In the inventory of the estate of the Loyalist, Hon. James Delancey of Annapolis, made in September 1804, there are listed ten old Windsor chairs valued at £1.1.0; and the inventory of the estate of Peter Shaw of Falmouth in 1817 included one dozen Windsor chairs valued at £4.

Cutter and Power, "Windsor Chair-Makers," were advertising in the *Acadian Recorder* of 1814 that "they still continue to carry on the above Business in the shop belonging to Abraham Cunard, opposite his Lumber Wharf, near the Dock-Yard" in Halifax. Abraham Cunard, was the father of Sir Samuel Cunard, the founder of the Cunard Steamship Line.

J. Cole of Halifax advertised in October 1816 that he was making Windsor and Grecian chairs "in the neatest and most durable manner" and also repairing and painting old chairs.

As very few craftsmen signed their chairs, we can usually only guess whether they are of local or foreign manufacture. I was fortunate in securing for the Provincial Museum at Citadel Hill an iron chair brand used by George Cole, who is listed at Rawdon in Hants County in the census of 1838. This brand was heated and the maker's name burned on the bottom of the chair seat. The value of a chair is considerably increased by branding, for we not only learn the maker's name but may be able to identify the year of manufacture.

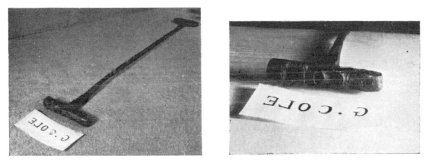

No. 24. Iron chair brand used by George Cole (1832-1859) of Centre Rawdon, Hants County. PHOTO BY E. LONGARD for the Provincial Museum Collection, Citadel Hill, Halifax, N.S.

It is probable that the J. Cole advertising as "Windsor and Grecian Chair Maker" at Halifax in 1816 was the James Cole who made chairs in Rawdon in the 1820's and 1830's, because Halifax was the traditional market for products from that part of Hants County. A birch Windsor armchair marked

"J. Cole" on the under-side of the wooden seat was made by James Cole about 1834. The six spindles are flat instead of round, and are turned to a smaller size where they join the narrow top rail.

James Cole, chairmaker, is said to have come to Nova Scotia from the United States, although the family claims to be Scottish. He lived first at Preston, Halifax County. By 1817 he was living in Rawdon township in Hants County, for a son was buried there in June of that year. He had at least seven children.

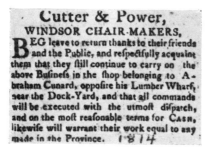

No. 25. Advertisements of Cutter & Power and J. Cole.

His son George was born about 1808, and died on March 29, 1859. On January 26, 1832, at St. Paul's Anglican Church at Centre Rawdon, he married Mary Ann Haley, a daughter of John and Sarah (Mason) Haley of South Rawdon, and the couple had a family of nine. George Cole carried on his father's business as chairmaker, but his chairs reveal slight differences. If he followed the pattern for the frame used by his father, the seat would be a different shape. One of his straight chairs is very graceful, with a bow back and widened top rail. It has five inner spindles (where the father's arm chair has six), and a rounded wooden seat (where his father's has a square saddle seat). Another armchair by George Cole has rounded spindles and back, flattened in front for comfort. His chairs are marked "G. COLE, WARRANTED." Cole chairs may be found in Musquodoboit, Maitland, Rawdon, Mount Uniacke and Windsor.

One of the earliest marked chairs was made by Degant who worked in Halifax in 1780. (See illustration No. 26). George Gammon of Dartmouth

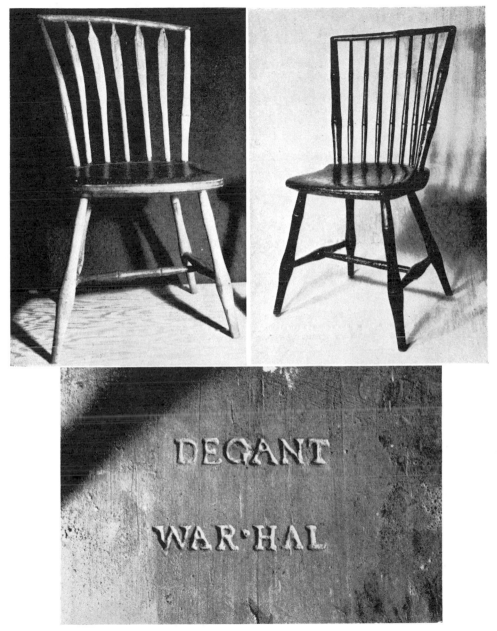

No. 26. Two types of Windsor chairs made by Degant who worked in Halifax as early as 1780. From the Provincial Museum *left* and the C. R. K. Allen Collection, Halifax *right*. The illustration *below* shows the Degant chair brand used on the chair seat. PHOTO BY E. LONGARD.

made a Windsor armchair which is also stamped. He called it a betrothal chair, having set a carved heart into the central back rung. This is marked "G. GAMMON warranted."

About 1859 George Gammon had a workshop on the road to Lawrence-town in Halifax County, and made chairs and tables, rocking chairs and spool beds. He used a wooden hand-made balance wheel, loaded with lead. Where decoration was required, the cutting was done by hand with chisels. In his workshop women and girls from the neighbourhood made eel-grass mattresses to sell to sailing ships.

No. 27. Two types of chairs made by George Gammon of Halifax about 1838. The armchair, in the collection of Mrs. W. H. Strachan, Halifax, is assumed to be a betrothal chair because of the carved heart set in the chair back. Both chairs are branded.

No. 28. *Upper left:* Pictou county chair owned by Mr. S. MacLaren, Pictou, Halifax. *Upper right:* Halifax county chair owned by Mr. C. R. K. Allen, Halifax, N.S. *Lower left:* Windsor chair made of birch, said to have been used by H.R.H. the Duke of Kent in the Theatre Royal in Halifax from 1794 to 1800. Now in the Masonic Hall, Halifax. *Lower right:* Spenser chair, Hants County, owned by Mrs. Harold Reid, Shubenacadie. PHOTOS BY E. LONGARD.

Upon investigation, one finds that most chairs made in Nova Scotia followed the Windsor pattern, except that the chair seat was of pine instead of oak.

One of the most popular chairs in the United States during the early nineteenth century was the Hitchcock chair. This was a variant of the slat-back manufactured in Connecticut by Lambert Hitchcock. It was a plain chair of which only the front legs and front rungs were turned, but to offset this simplicity the back was decorated with a fancy stencilled design in gilt and other colours. The women and children who worked in the Hitchcock factory applied designs of horns of plenty, fruit and leaf patterns and fountains with drinking birds by dipping their bare fingers first in linseed oil and then in red or blue colouring or in gold or bronze until their fingers became as stiff as boards.

Hitchcock priced his chairs at a dollar and a half, and in 1826 he built a large brick factory to handle additional orders. He probably sold some of his stock in the Maritimes, and his chairs are easily identifiable because he imprinted his name underneath the chair seats.

Local craftsmen in Nova Scotia were soon producing chairs in the Hitchcock style. In February 1831 Edward Heffernan was reminding his customers that his "stock is well seasoned, and of the best quality; and as he imports no Chairs from the United States, he can recommend his as very superior to any made by machinery."

At the same time Charles P. Allen was announcing that he had on hand in Halifax three hundred bottom chairs of various kinds and colours "warranted superior to any imported from Boston." Allen had "erected a Turning Lathe on Fall River, ten miles from Dartmouth, for the purpose of turning Chair Stock" and hoped to offer chairs for sale at prices lower than those imported from the United States. Twelve of his chairs could be packed compactly and shipped in one barrel. The lathe was driven by a water wheel situated on the falls below Miller Lake. Later he manufactured other types of furniture including settees and benches, and also had a bucket factory. In 1848 Charles P. Allen of Dartmouth became a British citizen by taking the

Oath of Allegiance to Queen Victoria, so presumably he had come to Nova Scotia from the United States.

In the *Halifax Sun* of November 26, 1849, C. P. Allen announced that recent rains had set his pail mill going again, and that he had reduced the prices of his chairs twenty per cent. "A good warranted Windsor Chair can be had now at my shop for 3 s. each, and on all other kinds the same reduction will be made for cash." Later Allen built a fine house called Waverley after Sir Walter Scott's popular novels, and became the founder of a village with the same name. One of his daughters married Peter Spriggs, who afterwards managed the Allen factory, and another daughter married Cornelius Blois, who had been apprenticed as a chairmaker to Charles P. Allen.

### SIBLEY CHAIRS

In Nova Scotia the Sibley name is identified with the manufacture of fine chairs. The family came to Nova Scotia in 1749; on the passenger list of the transport *Beaufort* arriving at Halifax in that year appears the name of Henry Sibley, soapmaker, accompanied by his wife and two sons.

A son of Henry, Stephen Sibley, moved from Halifax to carve a farm out of the forest at Wittenburg, situated in a valley near Stewiacke. Wittenburg had a brook that could produce power for mills and for turning lathes, while birch and pine for manufacturing furniture were easily procured from the neighbouring hills. There Stephen's third son, Joseph Sibley (born in 1790) earned the local title of "the chair maker" and made many other articles needed in the home such as looms and spinning wheels.

Joseph's eldest son, Shelomith, became interested in the manufacture of yarn and cloth. A contemporary of his, John Wright, has written that when Shelomith was visiting in New England he espied a woollen mill. A notice over the door read: "No admittance, except on business." He knew that inside the mill were secrets well worth guarding, because this was before 1870 and the days of patent rights. Nevertheless, this insignificant little stooped man with the perpetual grin knocked at the door of that mill and was admitted. A foreman even showed him around and answered all his innocent questions. When told what "this little thing" was for, or "that queer little object" was, Shelomith's only comment was "Umph." He was much interested in the machinery, and when he had seen all and was about to leave he thanked the foreman and said: "I guess I can make one like it." And that is just what he did.

Shelomith returned to Nova Scotia and built a woollen loom, said to have been the first in Pictou County. The Rev. Kennedy Wainwright of Stewiacke has information that on his New England tour Shelomith visited a factory making Venetian blinds where he studied the type of loom used in weaving the slats together. This he also made for use in the Sibley factory. His next move was to Truro, where he interested a Mr. Crowe in establishing an iron foundry, which was known as Sibley and Crowe. Later, on selling out, he moved to Stewiacke where he established the Stewacke Iron and Stove Foundry. Today his stoves are eagerly sought by hunters and fishermen to heat their lodges.

It was Michael Sibley, the fourth son of Joseph Sibley, who took over his father's woodworking shop and made chairs and spinning wheels. The slats of these Sibley chairs are curved, the frames are of birch, and the knobs are all of the same pattern. The seats are of "splints" or "splits." To make these the trunks of the black ash trees were cut and barked, then beaten by a pole axe on every part of the trunk until a layer could be stripped off, then another and another of each year's growth, until the required quantity was obtained. The layer thus split off was steamed until pliable enough to weave into chair bottoms. When ash trees became scarce in the district, later generations of Sibleys made chairs with wooden bottoms and stamped or burnt their names beneath the seat.

An infinite variety of slat-backs, from plain ones with two or three slats to handsome chairs having up to eight arched slats, were made as arm chairs or side chairs. The front and rear uprights were turned, simply or elaborately, according to the skill of the craftsman or the taste of his client. Most slat-backs were made of a variety of hardwoods—maple for the uprights, birch or ash for slats, and hickory or ash for stretchers.

Michael Sibley decided to enlarge his shop, and about 1856 built himself a water-wheel and mill where he manufactured two sizes of straight chairs,

No. 29. Sibley chairs. In the collection of Richard Sibley, Wittenburg, Colchester County, N.S. *Upper left:* Earliest type of Sibley chair, with woven seat and narrow slat back with the distinguishing turned finial. The background is an example of their manufacture of the woven Venetian blind. *Upper right:* A birch rocker with three wide slats, known as "Father's chair." *Lower left:* A birch rocking chair with four-slat back and a renewed woven cowhide seat instead of a splint bottom. It is known as "Mother's chair" and has shorter arms than "Father's chair." *Lower right:* Richard Sibley with one of the chairs made by his ancestors.

two sizes of rocking chairs (split bottomed), bedsteads, bureaus, spinning wheels, swifts and tables. His brother William wove the rustic Venetian blinds made of splint.

Michael employed a number of his Sibley cousins in the factory—among them Richard, Benjamin and Aaron. An old account book begun in 1855 by Michael Sibley records a working agreement with his cousin Benjamin, who must have been quite young and living at home. It is dated September 9, 1869. "Benjamin Sibley has hired with me for two years. The first year for the sum of Ten Cents per day or thirty dollars and thirty cents the year. And the second year for the sum of twenty cents per day to work in the shop and to make chairs and whatsoever may be in the way that could be called shop work. Payment to be made at the end of each year or otherwise as may suit."

Eventually Michael Sibley sold his factory at Wittenburg to his cousins Richard, Benjamin, Aaron, Stephen, Edward George, William and Ezekiel Thomas Sibley. Ezekiel Thomas became the president of the firm. A natural leader and organizer, he once remarked: "They say that conceit is half the battle. Well, if that be so, Zeke will do the other half."

Sibley Brothers enlarged the business and in 1878 were making Venetian blinds, split blinds, shutters, rocking horses, children's rocking chairs, sleds, wheelbarrows, stands, organ stools, tables, spool bedsteads, a double rocker, desks, bookcases and—of course—chairs. They did not make splint-bottomed chairs but made several sizes of straight chairs and rocking chairs with wooden seats. "Sibley Bros. Lower Stewiacke" was stamped in black ink on the chair and probably on other articles, for although the furniture was made in Wittenburg it was shipped from the railway station at Lower Stewiacke. This plant ceased operations about 1900.

Today nothing remains in Wittenburg of the Sibley factory, but the Sibley chair has stood the test of time. The ladder-back chairs and rockers are still in use in the valleys of the Stewiacke, Shubenacadie and Musquodoboit, where collectors eagerly seek them out. The distinguishing feature of these chairs is the fine turning of the chair-back, surmounted with a turning that is strictly a Sibley innovation. Another clue to identification is that most Sibley chairs are stamped with a stencil on the wooden bottom.

No. 30. Later Sibley chairs. *Left;* A child's rocker made by the Sibleys. From the collection of the Provincial Museum. The later Sibley chairs had seats made of pine under which the Sibley label was stencilled. *Centre:* A Sibley side chair with pine seat. From the Provincial Museum Collection. *Right:* A late addition to the Sibley line, the spandrel back chair with woven cane seat with a grained imitation mahogany finish.

## BASS RIVER CHAIRS

If a man has good corn, or wood, or boards, or pigs to sell, or can make better chairs or knives, crucibles, or church organs, than anybody else, you will find a broad, hard-beaten road to his house, tho' it be in the woods.                                          *Emerson.*

In the pioneer days of Nova Scotia there came to the province a young surveyor named James Fulton. Having qualified as a land surveyor Fulton had emigrated in 1760 from Londonderry, Ireland, to New England, where he followed his profession for five years. Then he was sent to help survey the province of Nova Scotia, and as part compensation he was awarded in 1768 a grant of land in the district now known as Bass River in Colchester County.

Two of his descendants, George and William Fulton, were carpenters who built houses in summer and made furniture in winter. In 1859 they built a sawmill near the mouth of Bass River. By 1860 George had installed an automatic attachment to reverse the carriage of the "home-made" jack-knife saw, and was turning wood for bedsteads and other furniture on a lathe. After a decade of operations on a small scale, William decided that the business should be removed to Truro, the railway centre fourteen miles away. George refused to join his brother, and the partnership was dissolved.

About this time the Acadia chair factory at Portaupique, five miles from Bass River, came up for sale at sheriff's auction. George Fulton bought the factory for the sum of two thousand dollars and moved the machinery to Bass River. There he began the manufacture of chairs on a larger scale, selling the products almost exclusively in the Maritime Provinces. Soon he was making other lines of furniture, and the business continued to grow in spite of competition from the factories of "Upper" Canada after the Intercolonial Railway had been completed in 1876.

When the first factory was destroyed by fire on March 17, 1885, it was decided to build a four-storey building costing $24,500 and to specialize in the making of chairs.

Today the Bass River chairs made by the Dominion Chair Company are known all over Canada and in the West Indies, Ireland, Australia, New Zealand and South Africa, although the plant has been destroyed by fire five times—March 17, 1885; November 3, 1892; December 31, 1909; November 23, 1940; and July 27, 1948. Among the most popular of the thirty different types of tables and chairs currently being produced are college chairs with writing arm, school desks, swivel chairs, guest chairs, Windsor bow-backed armchairs, chairs for assembly and church halls, offices, schools and kindergartens, high-backed auditorium chairs, and "World's Champion" rockers.

MAHOGANY CHAIRS

Good examples of carved mahogany chairs made in Halifax in the mid-nineteenth century are those to be seen in the Red Chamber of the Province House at Halifax, which was used by the Legislative Council of Nova Scotia

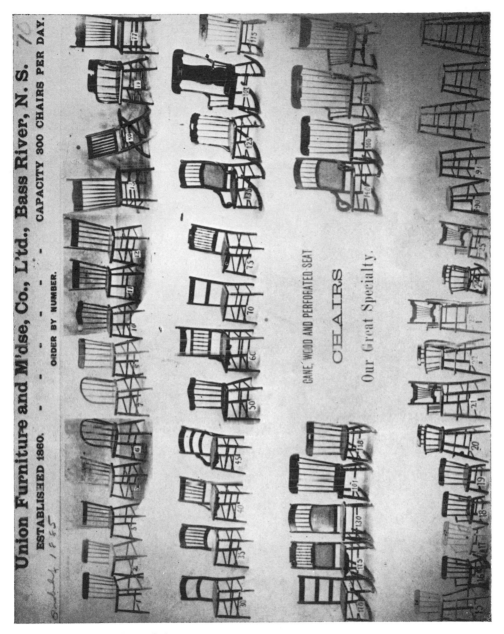

No. 31. Bass River chairs. PHOTO COURTESY OF THE BASS RIVER CHAIR CO., BASS RIVER, N.S.

until its abolition in 1928. These chairs were made by George MacLeod, whose father emigrated from Scotland to Pictou County. George had a workshop at Cross Roads in Pictou County, near Mount Thom, before moving to Halifax. Although he made some mahogany furniture, he was better known as a carver of figure heads for vessels.

Twenty-one of the chairs used by the Legislative Councillors have a beautifully carved crown on the cresting, plain arms, and a carved lion's mask and sprays of mayflowers on the front of the seat rail, two modified claw feet with carving on the knees, and plain cabriole rear legs. These chairs, originally upholstered in horsehair, are now covered with red velvet.

No. 32. *Left:* Legislative Councillor's mahogany chair. *Right:* Chair of the President of the Legislative Council of Nova Scotia. Both were made by George MacLeod of Halifax about 1858. PHOTOS BY ROBERT JONES.

One chair, used by the President of the Legislative Council, is an armchair with more elaborate carving than the chairs used by the Councillors. It has roses on the cresting instead of a crown, roses on the knees of the cabriole legs, and roses instead of the lion mask on the front rail. The window casings, door frames and ceiling ornaments of the Red Chamber have motifs of lions' heads, thistles, shells and vines.

Two other splendid chairs to be seen in the Red Chamber are the Royal Chairs standing on the dais at the west end of the room. The King's Chair stands before Allan Ramsay's portrait of King George III. It has a very high cresting, elaborately carved with a crown and rose, thistle, shamrock and mayflower enclosed in scrolls, lion's claw feet, arms ending in lions' heads, heavy carving on the knee, and a shell and roses on the front rail. The back legs are plain but curved.

The Queen's Chair stands before Ramsay's portrait of Queen Charlotte and the carved crown copies the one to be seen in the painting. King George III and Queen Charlotte were reigning when the Province House was opened in 1819.

The first Royal Chair was made at New York by John Henry Belter, the noted cabinetmaker, for the visit of the Prince of Wales (later King Edward VII) to Halifax in August 1860. Belter had been excellently trained in cabinet making and wood carving in his native Germany before he emigrated to New York. The lace-like and deeply-cut carving characteristic of his furniture was the produce of carvers trained in Alsace-Lorraine or the Black Forest.

Working only in rosewood, Belter invented a method of laminating this wood that made it possible for him to create a unique style of handsomely carved and pierced chairs with concave backs. He made drawing room suites for wealthy New Yorkers from 1844 to 1865; today his furniture is scarce and costly. Belter collaborated with the founder of the Steinway piano firm, devising for him the method of laminating rounded front corners of square piano cases and designing the heavy cabriole legs needed to support the weight of these instruments.

A companion Royal Chair was needed for the visit of H.M. King George VI and H.M. Queen Elizabeth to Halifax in June 1939. This was constructed and carved in twenty-seven days in 1939 by Mr. Alexander Herman MacMillan of Halifax from choice Honduras mahogany, using over fifty tools. Experts at that time said that his work on the royal chair could not be surpassed anywhere in the world.

A. H. MacMillan is the son of the late John D. MacMillan of New Glasgow, an ornamental plasterer. After manual training in that town he

No. 33. Royal chairs at Province House, Halifax. *Left:* Chair made in New York in 1860 by the noted John H. Belter, successor to Duncan Phyffe. It had been commissioned by the Province of Nova Scotia for the visit in 1860 of the Prince of Wales, later King Edward VII. *Right:* Chair constructed and carved by Mr. A. Herman MacMillan of Halifax in 1939 of choice Honduras mahogany. It was commissioned by the Province of Nova Scotia to match the original, the occasion being the visit to Halifax in June, 1939 of H. M. King George VI and H. M. Queen Elizabeth.   PHOTOS BY ROBERT JONES.

No. 34. A splint bottom chair made by the "Cape Breton Chairmaker," the late E. H. Hart of North-East Margaree, in 1958; a maple stool made by "Chip" Smith of Chester in the same year; and a mat woven in Nova Scotia. PHOTO BY E. LONGARD at the N.S. Handcraft Centre at Halifax.

went to the United States as a pattern maker. He settled in Halifax in 1919, and has served the city as alderman and as deputy mayor in 1953-1954. His first woodcarving was a tuna fishing trophy to be presented at the first annual tuna angling cup matches at Wedgeport in 1937. He also carved the coat-of-arms hanging in the Halifax City Council Chamber.

# CHAPTER FOUR

# Furniture Factories

A number of furniture factories flourished in Nova Scotia in the nineteenth century. Of these perhaps the best known are A. Stephen and Son and Gordon and Keith of Halifax, John Bath Reed of Bridgetown, and John Cumming of New Glasgow, and of course that of the Dominion Chair Company of Bass River.

The furniture produced adheres to Victorian or American Empire styles. Although these styles are not admired by the present generation, we should acknowledge the fine quality of the materials and the workmanship in the early Victorian period from 1837 to 1850. In the mid-Victorian period, from 1850 to 1875, the rosewood or mahogany of the early years of the reign were superseded by black walnut with coarse or grotesque carvings. The chairs are in better taste, however, than other articles.

It will be recalled that in 1831 Charles P. Allen had established a turning lathe on Fall River, near Waverley, about ten miles from Dartmouth, in an attempt to produce enough chairs to meet American competition. Subsequently five other mills were built on the river by William and James Spriggs, Sewell W. Brittan, Malcom and Stephen. Brittan, who had been born in Massachusetts, had come to Nova Scotia in 1831, and had engaged in business as a chairmaker and turner on the Truro Road (Waverley) since 1835. In 1847 he became a British citizen. He made a large armchair especially for his wife who was a huge woman, and it was long admired in the community. All the mills used water power from the falls to turn their lathes and saws. In 1861 the district had one furniture manufacturer and four chairmakers.

Alexander Stephen, a native of Rothes, Scotland, came to Nova Scotia when he was about fifteen. After clerking for a short time in a grocery store in Halifax, he moved to Musquodoboit where he purchased a farm and married Mary Guild. By 1845, when their son Alexander was born, the family were living in Halifax where the senior Alexander was a partner in the wholesale grocery firm of John Esson and Company. He was also a prominent member of the North British Society, serving as president in 1867.

About 1862 Alexander Stephen left the grocery trade for the furniture business. The junior Alexander became a partner in the firm, which under the name of A. Stephen and Son began to manufacture furniture on a limited scale at Fall River and Musquodoboit.

Early in the 1860's an enterprising German capitalist, Franz von Ellershausen, had purchased 3000 acres of wilderness about forty miles from Halifax along the railway line to Windsor. Thirty German families emigrated to Nova Scotia to work for him, cleared 300 acres and raised crops of wheat and sugar beet. The village of Ellershausen soon contained thirty-two houses, four stores, hotels and two mills. Ellershausen and his family lived in "an elegant three-storey house" that was the admiration of the countryside.

"Baron" Ellershausen secured about 12,000 acres of timberland on the Ponhook Lakes at the head of the St. Croix River, and mill sites on the river. Three-quarters of a mile above Ellershausen station he erected a watermill 140 feet long, 44 feet wide, and three storeys high, and there installed machines for cutting logs and deals, lathes and buckets. The saws and other apparatus were driven by a water wheel sixteen feet in diameter, with a length of upwards of fifteen feet.

Ellershausen made unsuccessful speculations in a copper mine in Newfoundland and lost his fortune; the crops on his estate were a failure, and most of the German families moved away. In 1866 he disposed of the steam mills and a great part of his timberlands to Alexander Stephen and Son. This company obtained immediate returns on their investment by manufacturing lumber for the British market, and by making buckets and other woodenware from deal ends and other waste. Thomas Archibald supervised the thirty men employed by the company.

Shortly afterwards Alexander Stephen and Son began the production of pine furniture, and in the *Morning Chronicle* of June 1, 1868, they were advertising that in their factory at Ellershouse "they have all the necessary facilities to enable them to produce a superior article at a very low price. Having secured the services of the best mechanics to be procured in the Provinces and the United States, we are enabled to produce Furniture which for durability and style of finish will rank equal, if not superior, to any made in the United States or elsewhere."

They had on hand parlour suites in walnut; chamber sets in pine, chestnut and walnut; cane and wood seat chairs of every description; bedsteads in Swiss, cottage, round-cornered and French patterns; and they had received from the Ellerhouse factories twenty-five oak extension tables, six, eight and ten feet long, that were "superior to the imported Chestnut or Walnut."

At the Provincial Agricultural and Industrial Exhibition of Nova Scotia held at Halifax in October 1868, A. Stephen and Son were awarded several prizes. They won first prize of $15 and second prize of $8 for bedroom furniture, consisting of a bedstead, bureau and glass, four chairs with cane seats, towel horse, wash stand and rocker, all made of wood native to Canada. These were probably all of the spool type. The firm also won a prize of $6 for the best couch, and of $8 for the best mangle or wringer.

When St. Andrew's Presbyterian Church of Halifax moved to their new edifice on Tobin Street in 1871, the Stephen firm purchased the building on the southeast corner of Barrington and Prince Streets where the T. Eaton Company is now located, and renovated it as a modern furniture shop.

In 1881 A. Stephen and Son were advertising their rattan goods, being "the sole manufacturers of these articles in the Dominion. This is a new enterprise on our part; but our facilities for manufacturing them cannot be surpassed outside the United States. To all who wish to encourage *Home Manufactures,* our *Exhibit* in this *Department* cannot fail to prove worthy of inspection."

Alexander Stephen, jr., continued the firm after his father's death in 1884 until 1890, when it became a limited liability company under the name of the Nova Scotia Furnishing Company. In 1909 it occupied an imposing six-storey building at 72-76 Barrington Street, which had been opened in 1894, but there is no mention of the manufacture of furniture by this firm. Competition from central Canada and the United States had finally forced the company to stop local manufacture.

No. 35. Furniture warehouse of A. Stephen & Son, on southeast corner of Prince and Barrington Streets, Halifax, in 1875. St. Andrew's Presbyterian Church occupied this site from 1818 to 1871. When the congregation moved to a new church in 1871, the building was purchased and renovated by Alexander Stephen & Son. Later it was occupied by Miller Bros. and Mahon's Limited, and razed by T. Eaton & Co. in 1928 to make way for their department store. COURTESY G. W. HAZEN, HALIFAX, N.S.

Gordon and Keith were the successors of Thomson and Esson, who had been doing business in Halifax in the 1820's and were for many years the leading cabinetmakers of the city.

James Thomson, the founder of the firm, was one of the signers of the Cabinetmakers' Protest of 1826. In that year the partnership of Charles Alexander and James Thomson was dissolved, and James Thomson, cabinetmaker, removed from Hollis Street, opposite the Province House, to No. 51 Barrington Street, opposite Hon. S. B. Robie's. Like so many other cabinetmakers, he also carried on the business of undertaker, promising "funerals carefully conducted on moderate terms." A native of Pennycuik in the Midlothian district of Scotland, Thomson became an active member of the North British Society. He was interested in education and literature, a supporter of the Halifax Library and president of the Mechanics' Institute.

In the Public Archives of Nova Scotia there is a mahogany Victorian armchair similar to those in the Red Chamber at Province House. It has the lion mask on the seat rail, but no mayflowers, and has a crown on the cresting. This chair was presented to the Archives in 1935 by Mrs. A. J. White, who said that it had been made by her grandfather James Thomson and that the Prince of Wales (later King Edward VII) had sat in it during his visit to Halifax in 1860.

In 1854 James Thomson was one of the judges for manufactures in wood at the first exhibition held in Nova Scotia. Among the prizes awarded were £2 to Thomson and Esson for a ship's wheel, and £1 for a mahogany music stool. The Esson in this partnership was George Esson, senior, born in Aberdeen, who died at Musquodoboit Harbour on January 2, 1886, aged seventy-seven.

At the same exhibition James Gordon was given prizes of £3 for the second best walnut sofa, and of £1.10.0 for the second best set of half a dozen drawing-room chairs, and a diploma and fifteen shillings for a fancy mahogany table. He carried on business as a cabinetmaker and upholsterer at 123 Barrington Street, south of Saint Paul's Church.

In 1860 James Gordon and Donald Keith purchased the furniture business of Thomson and Esson. Donald Keith was another Scot, born in Thurso on October 10, 1832. His father, John Keith, had emigrated to Halifax, where he found employment as a brewer. Donald served his apprenticeship in cabinetmaking with Fielding and Ulman of Halifax, and then worked in

Wolfville and Windsor, before returning to Halifax for employment with Thomson and Esson. About 1882 he bought James Gordon's share. For a time J. E. G. Bolton was a partner, and then Alexander Keith, a nephew of Donald. In 1896 Donald Keith retired, to be succeeded by Alexander Keith.

No. 36. Trade label of James Gordon. COURTESY OF THE PUBLIC ARCHIVES OF NOVA SCOTIA.

Large factories were unusual in the Maritimes in the 1860's, because the tariff was light and the local manufacturer found it difficult to compete successfully with the American producer who enjoyed an almost unlimited market for the products of his machinery. Later Confederation was blamed for this situation, as Ontario proved to be centrally located for markets throughout the whole Dominion of Canada.

On the first page of the *Novascotian* newspaper of November 2, 1863, appeared a description of Gordon and Keith's furniture factory. It was situated a short distance off the eastern side of Queen Street, to the rear of the General's residence, and the street was named Dundonald after Donald Keith. The laundry of the Halifax Infirmary now occupies the site, and the General's residence has become the property of the Nova Scotia Technical College.

The factory was a storey and a half high, with many windows, and a six horsepower engine on the ground floor drove the machinery. The reporter described in detail the operation of the circular saw, cut-off saw, surface planing machine, two jig-saws, a steam lathe and a foot lathe. "With these lathes are executed all the turning required for use in the factory, comprising pedestals for centre tables, desk legs, ordinary table legs, and a variety of other articles requisite in the trade." Large stocks of seasoned mahogany, walnut, chestnut, pine and mahogany veneer were kept on hand.

No. 37. A Notman plate showing Gordon & Keith's furniture factory on Dundonald Street, Halifax, looking south to St. Luke's Anglican Church. COURTESY OF THE PUBLIC ARCHIVES OF NOVA SCOTIA.

Thomas Connors, a carver at Gordon and Keith's, described the processes. He gave high praise to the firm's workmanship for, he said, "their work was made to last." The parts of a piece of furniture, such as the legs of a table, were carved separately with chisels and hammers and special knives. When the carving was complete, the pieces were handed over to the joiner. The upholsterers and finishers had their separate tasks. The blocked side-front pieces were glued or dowelled on, while top-rails, with their carved fruit or flowers, were kept in place by dowels over the horsehair upholstery. In 1863 about thirty men were employed in making mahogany and walnut sofas, chairs, couches, bookcases, bedsteads and centre tables. Chestnut was used for bedsteads and other bedroom furniture.

Gordon and Keith made wardrobes and chairs for the Halifax Hotel, which was demolished in April 1948, a sideboard and chairs for the City Club, and pews for St. James' Presbyterian Church in Dartmouth. The firm also supplied furniture for many ships built in Nova Scotia. The four-masted barquentine *Ensenada,* which was launched at South Maitland, was equipped with furniture made by Gordon and Keith "to their own designs." The cabins were roomy and airy, finished in polished ash, oak and cherry.

In 1867 the factory on Dundonald Street was destroyed by fire. It was rebuilt in brick, 105 x 40 feet and three storeys high, to produce furniture to display in the handsome warerooms at 41-45 Barrington Street. This building was spacious and well ventilated, and in 1883 it was refitted with the most modern machinery at a cost of $5,000.

Twenty years later, on Sunday morning August 21, 1887, a policeman discovered a fire in the factory. The summer had been very dry, and because of a shortage of water the building was again destroyed. The loss was over $25,000, covered by only $4,000 insurance. All summer fifty workmen had been making stock for the fall trade; one hundred ash bedroom suites, together with other furniture valued at $8,000, had been completed and would have been removed on Monday to the warehouse.

Each workman lost tools worth from twenty-five to one hundred dollars. William Coombes, foreman, Stewart Naufts, John Harvey, Edward Ward, William Misener, George Morton and William Locke had been employed by Gordon and Keith for over twenty years. John and James Misener "were master-workmen, their carving a true art, the very best." They made mahogany easy chairs, side chairs, a mahogany sofa, fine mahogany Pembroke tables, a checkerboard table with inlaid squares of black walnut and white bird's eye maple, and a handsome tip-table made of "plum-pudding" or "burr" mahogany. John Misener also made cabinets for pianos, being associated with Thomas Brockley and Company of Halifax.

Immediately Donald Keith rebuilt the factory on Dundonald Street. In 1896 he erected for $70,000 an imposing stone four-storey shop and warehouse, now the Green Lantern Building on Barrington Street. It was fireproof, built of freestone, brick and granite in a romanesque style. No modern conveniences were missed for it was "wired for electricity, piped for gas, and heated with hot water."

Like A. Stephen and Son, Gordon and Keith eventually found it impossible to compete in furniture manufacture, but the retail activities of the firm are still carried on by the Alexander Keith Furniture Company in the Bayers Road Shopping Centre in Halifax.

Gordon and Keith submitted to the International Exhibition of 1862 at London a drawing-room centre table, a chiffonier, two couches, and a drawing-room chair—all in walnut and all in the Cinquecento arabesque style.

McEwan and Reid of Halifax exhibited at the International Exhibition of 1862 at London a sofa of native oak covered in green Utrecht velvet, the elbows being supported by dolphins; an easy chair featuring the kingfisher (the emblem of the city of Halifax); a small chair for a library; a maple drawing-room chair made of wood from the Duke of Kent's estate at Prince's Lodge; and an Elizabethan cabinet of nine native woods.

John Bath Reed of Bridgetown in Annapolis County sent two prize-winning bedroom sets and one parlour suite to the Agricultural and Industrial Exhibition at Halifax in 1880. Mrs. Elizabeth Ruggles Coward described one massive bedroom suite thus in her *History of Bridgetown*: It "was of solid black walnut, heavily carved and moulded, with columns and raised panels of French Walnut Beryl beautifully polished and mounted with polished slabs of white marble from Messrs. Falconer and Whitman . . . the head of the bed and the top of the bureau almost touched the ceiling." The parlour furniture was of "walnut upholstered in silk brocatelle of a rich crimson colour, with piped back and puffed and corded edges." The designer was James DeForrest, and Thomas Kelly and Mr. Zwicker assisted him.

At that time Mr. Reed charged $60 to $120 for parlour suites, $25 to $40 for pine bedroom suites, $19 to $24 for sofas, and $3 to $6 for walnut chairs. A solid walnut centre table was priced at $10, and when surmounted by an "elegant marble top" brought as much as $16. It was fashionable to place a table in the exact centre of the parlour, with a large family Bible on it.

James DeForrest also designed and carved a set of black walnut chairs for the new Masonic Hall at Annapolis Royal, and two fluted and bronzed Corinthian pillars to accompany the chairs.

John Reed had started cabinetmaking for himself in 1858 in a small room over a shop in Bridgetown. In 1876 his steam cabinet factory employed only ten men, but the business expanded steadily until 1890. At first all labour was done by hand, but the purchase of a four-horsepower engine enabled Reed to compete with the American furniture then being brought into the country. Fire, the usual enemy of furniture makers, destroyed his factory, but he built a brick house twenty-two feet square for a new twenty-horsepower engine that ran a dozen engines.

Probably John Bath Reed had served his apprenticeship with John Emslie, one of the better known cabinetmakers of the district, as early as 1833. In 1857 Reed and Emslie were advertising furniture for sale, including a chair in the "Jenny Lind Pattern."

One day, about the year 1860, John Emslie and the local doctor were driving past a pile of trees that had been cut for firewood from the estate of General Timothy Ruggles, an old Loyalist. The cabinetmaker noticed the colour of the wood of one large tree, and halted to examine it. Ruggles had imported many trees and flowers from the United States and planted them in a sheltered gulch on the mountainside. The cabinetmaker purchased the tree—a magnificent specimen of black walnut—and sent it to the sawmill. One piece of furniture made from it was a chair owned for many years by the Woodbury family.

John Cumming opened a steam operated factory in New Glasgow about 1868. As a young man he had emigrated to New England where he worked in factories and acquired a knowledge of business and practical mechanics. Then he returned to Pictou County where his brother William was operating a water powered furniture factory at Piedmont, producing spool beds on a small scale.

The Cumming factory used native woods such as birch, maple and pine, and imported walnut and mahogany. The birch and maple were stained a cherry colour, and the furniture made from this became very popular. The factory employed about a dozen men and some boy apprentices to produce both solid and veneer pieces. John Cumming is credited with the introduction of the first automatic wood turning machine into Nova Scotia, and he utilized his steam exhaust in an ingenious box contraption to bend chair backs and hockey sticks.

John Cumming arranged for the New Glasgow merchant William Mac-Intosh to bring back cloth for upholstering when he travelled to England for his own firm. This cloth was shipped by water in vessels which came up the East River to wharves in New Glasgow. As one might expect, much of the upholstering was horsehair. John Cumming's niece, Ann Cumming, did most of the designing on the painted headboards of beds and on other pieces. The bulk of the furniture produced in the Cumming factory was shipped by water to retailers in the United States. Mr. James M. Cameron in the *Industrial History of the New Glasgow District* has pointed out that the Cumming factory declined and finally closed about 1900 because it had been established on the ability to buy cheaply in Britain, and sell finished products in New England. After Confederation it was forced to buy its cloth in tariff-protected central Canada, and could not meet competition and sell its products after paying the freight charges by railway to Quebec and Ontario.

# CHAPTER FIVE

# Clocks

Technically clocks should not be classed as furniture, but as most collectors possess one or two examples, I am including some brief notes on clocks and their makers. A list of some Nova Scotian clockmakers may be found in Appendix F.

As Halifax was a naval base and a shipping centre, it was important to have competent artisans to regulate and repair chronometers and marine instruments. It was the American Revolution, however, that brought to Nova Scotia to practise their craft the earliest clock- and watchmakers of whom I have record. Charles Geddes, the Etter family and John Paget came to settle in Halifax, while Thomas Adams, Isaac Clemens, Isaac Reed, Dulcina Stoughton and Michael Weathers came as Loyalists to Shelburne.

At least one Nova Scotian clockmaker died a wealthy man, but he made his fortune from shipping speculations rather than by his regular business. Charles Geddes, a brother of Robert Geddes the cabinetmaker, joined his brother in Halifax in 1783. An advertisement in the *Nova Scotia Gazette* of September 2nd of that year stated that "Charles Geddes from London, lately from New York, has opened a shop in Granville St. . . . He hopes for encouragement from Gentlemen of the Navy and Army, and the Respectable Inhabitants of the Town and Province." During the Napoleonic wars Geddes accumulated a fortune by purchasing condemned prizes and cargoes captured from the French by the British fleet and sold by the Admiralty Court at Halifax. His estate was estimated to be worth £100,000.

In 1783 Charles Geddes joined the North British Society, becoming president in 1806. The Geddes brothers also belonged to the literary group that met weekly at the Pontac Inn. Members read papers on social and scientific subjects and then spent the rest of the evening in conversation, songs and toasts; the Duke of Kent sometimes joined them.

The Etter family had accompanied the British army to Halifax when Lord Howe evacuated Boston in March 1776. Peter Etter, junior, had probably been born in Braintree, Massachusetts, where his father was a weaver. On his arrival in Nova Scotia, he enlisted in the Royal Fencible American Regiment and served at Fort Cumberland. By 1781 he had opened a jewellery store in Halifax, and in December 1782 he was advertising himself as a watch- and clockmaker. About 1787 he removed to Westmorland County in New Brunswick, where he had received a grant of land. Opening a shop at Fort Cumberland, he carried on business as a watchmaker, jeweller and silversmith until 1798. His brother Benjamin Etter took over the Halifax business and continued it until 1813, when he retired in favour of his son-in-law, Thomas Hosterman.

Many of the tall or long-case clocks found in Nova Scotia were imported from Great Britain. The Reverend George Hill in his *Memoir of Sir Brenton Halliburton* says that in the homes of merchants and government officials in Halifax in the early decades of the nineteenth century in "almost every hall stood a clock, encased by a frame of great size; a custom introduced by the Germans, from whose native land they seem to have been imported in great numbers." The term grandfather clock did not become common until after the 1880's when the song "My Grandfather's Clock" swept Britain and America.

The Halifax cabinetmaking firm of Tulles, Pallister and M'Donald also made cases for tall clocks. One example of their fine workmanship may be seen at the Provincial Museum at Citadel Hill. This mahogany case is seven feet five inches high, with inlaid door and base. The label is the same as that in illustration No. 22. This clock was presented to the province of Nova Scotia by the estate of A. J. Parker of Shubenacadie.

No. 38. Tall clock made at Halifax, 1810-1812, by Tulles, Pallister and M'Donald. It has a mahogany case, inlaid door and base, and is 7′ 5″ high. Provincial Museum, Citadel Hill, Halifax. PHOTO BY E. G. L. WETMORE.

John Geddie, the noted Nova Scotian maker of tall clocks, was born in Banff, Scotland, about 1778, and died at West River in Pictou County on April 27, 1843. He served his apprenticeship in his native land and entered business as a clockmaker. Coming to Pictou to settle with his family in 1817, he produced clocks closely approaching those of England and Scotland in beauty of design and decoration. Dr. George Patterson, the Historian of Pictou County, says that Geddie made all the works himself, and painted the delicate decorations upon the dial plates. Others believe that Geddie imported works from Scotland although he made the cases with much skill and artistic taste.

The clock in the vestry of First Presbyterian Church in Pictou was made about 1832. It is six and a half feet high, and is made of the finest mahogany. The hood has on either side a cylindrical column with a neat brass base and capital. The broken pediment is gracefully designed. In the lunette is painted a hunting scene, showing a man on horseback, with a dog and a tree; and in each spandrel is a rose and leaves. Below the centre of the dial is a curved opening for a calendar dial. Mr. Geddie also made some clock cases of local pine. Dr. John Geddie, the celebrated missionary to the New Hebrides, was his son, and tradition says that he helped his father at clockmaking when he was a boy.

The Troup family of Halifax were noted clockmakers and silversmiths. Alexander Troup, senior, was born in 1776 and died in Halifax on December 30, 1856, aged eighty years. His son Alexander Troup, junior, was born in 1806 and died on October 8, 1873. Thomas Troup (1819-1877) also made clocks.

The lack of timepieces in Nova Scotia in the early decades of the nineteenth century is illustrated by a letter published in the *Colonial Patriot* of 1831 decrying the fact that the masters were working their men too long. In Pictou there were a number of master tradesmen employing two or three apprentices and as many journeymen "whom they keep at work, without the knowledge of any kind of hours at all." These men had to be at work as soon as it was light in the morning, go to their meals just when it suited the master's fancy, and then labour again as long as they could see. The correspondent

No. 39. John Geddie tall clock in the possession of Charles Underwood of Halifax.
PHOTO BY E. LONGARD.

urged that a town clock be erected to enable the oppressed journeymen and labourers to insist on regular hours for meals and quitting, otherwise they would leave town looking for a better set of employers. Even the cheapest clocks and watches available in Nova Scotia must have been beyond the means of labourers.

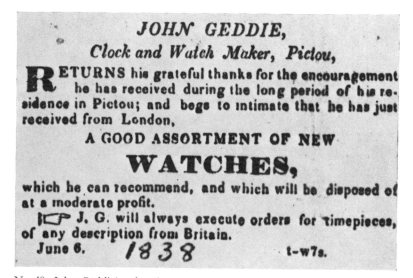

No. 40. John Geddie's advertisement.

After the War of 1812 Eli Terry of Connecticut had begun to produce wooden-works shelf clocks in quantity at a price within the reach of many clockless households. His thirty-hour clocks told time with fair accuracy, and the "pillar-and-scroll" case was popular with housewives. To the earlier box case were later added Sheraton details such as valanced bracket case, slender pillars, and scrolled pediment with brass urn finals or pineapples. This type of clock was popular for about thirty years.

Over one thousand movements for Terry's "improved" clock were made in the year 1820 alone at Plymouth Hollow, now Thomaston, in Connecticut. The plates of the movement were usually of oak, the wheels of apple or mahogany, the escape wheel only of brass. The dials were of painted wood, almost invariably eleven inches by eleven inches in size, and the spandrels were often rose painted in gilt and several contrasting colours.

At Clifton, the former home of Thomas Chandler Haliburton at Windsor, may be seen an Eli Terry clock that was made for George Steel of Horton and presented to this historic house many years later by the late Premier A. S. MacMillan.

Terry's movements were sometimes sold without their cases; these would be provided by local joiners or cabinetmakers. The cases made in Nova Scotia copied closely the style of the original, the glass panel below the dial being about seven inches by eleven, and painted with birds, flowers, fruit, or a domestic scene.

T. C. Haliburton, a Nova Scotian judge, became famous as the author of *The Clockmaker, Or the Sayings and Doings of Samuel Slick,* which was published in 1836. While Judge Haliburton was travelling around the province holding court he probably met a number of Yankees selling clocks in the country district, using plenty of "soft sawder" and "human natur" to charge more than the clocks were worth. Sam was selling clocks of the Eli Terry type. Haliburton said that he first met Sam Slick while the latter was on his "eastern circuit" somewhere between Colchester County and Fort Lawrence, near Amherst.

A well-known itinerant clockmaker of this district was Moses Barrett, who was born in New England about 1800 and came to Nova Scotia, where he plied his trade as clockmaker at Yarmouth and later at Amherst.

On exhibition in the Provincial Museum at Citadel Hill in Halifax are two examples of Moses Barrett's work. One is a shelf or mantelpiece "improved" wooden clock, probably a thirty-hour one of the Eli Terry type, manufactured at Yarmouth. This "Sam Slick clock" is thirty inches high from the base of the claw-shaped legs to the top of the pineapple finials. On the lower panel of the glass door is a crudely painted representation of a towered building or castle, with three trees and a rosebush. Inside the case is a printed label in three sections, the centre one reading: "Improved Clocks/

Warranted (design of rose and a thistle) if well used/Manufactured at Yarmouth, N.S./By/Moses Barrett (design of an eagle and palm leaves)/."

Moses Barrett imported the movements from Connecticut, and in winter made cases and assembled his clocks. For a time he lived two miles outside

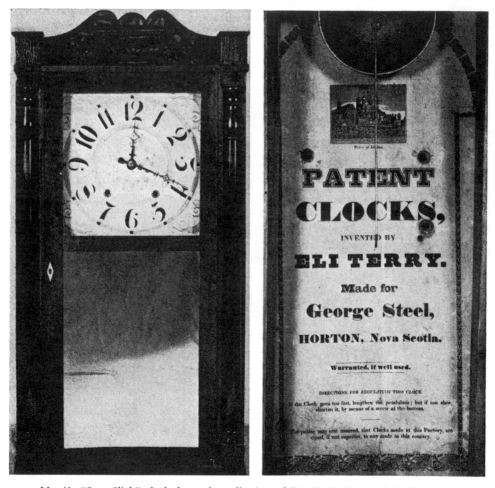

No. 41. "Sam Slick" clock from the collection of Dr. C. M. Jones of Halifax, and the label. PHOTOS BY WILLIAM WOOD.

Amherst in a house, later known as the Robert Barry house, in which he had his home, workshop and barn under one roof. In the summer he travelled around Nova Scotia selling his clocks, and Barrett clocks are to be found in Cumberland, Colchester, Pictou, Hants and Kings Counties. Barrett was always accompanied by his cat, which he could never bear to leave behind. When he stopped at a farmhouse he would assemble a clock, or mend an old one, and as part payment would receive his board and lodgings. He was a bachelor and "much preferred an uncut pumpkin pie for a serving, in fact he resented anything smaller being offered."

Apparently Moses Barrett was in partnership with another clockmaker by the name of Ladd, because the second clock in the Provincial Museum collection carries a label "Barrett and Ladd." Manufactured at Amherst, probably about 1835-1840, this is another typical "wooden-clock." The upright oblong case is of mahogany veneer over a pine backing, and on the back of the glass door before the pendulum is painted a crude representation of a large mansion with palmlike trees. The case is 31.30" by 16.60"; dial-plate 11.10" high by 11.60" wide; circular dial is 10.15" diameter; pendulum 16.75"; brass gong 4" in diameter with concave side to front; and painted glass in front of pendulum, 12.50" high and 9.70" wide. The well cut wooden wheels have steel pinions, escapement wheel and gong are of brass, two lead weights are wound up with a key, and the face is of enamelled wood with roman numerals and a crimson rose and leaves in each spandrel.

John McCulloch, a clockmaker of Halifax, made an unusual clock in the shape of the Sir Walter Scott Monument at Edinburgh, inside a glass case. This clock was made about 1850 and was exhibited at the Great London Exhibition of 1851 in the Crystal Palace. It was raffled in London the next year and won by William Smith of Bathurst, New Brunswick, who brought it back to this side of the Atlantic. It is now on display at the Public Archives of Nova Scotia, having been presented by George deBlois Smith.

John McCulloch was another Scot from Glasgow, but he learned his trade in Halifax as an apprentice to Peter Nordbeck. He was in business on his own account from 1844 until his death in 1875 as a goldsmith, manufacturing

No. 42. Barrett & Ladd clock made in Amherst, N.S., between 1835 and 1840. The
Provincial Museum, Citadel Hill, Halifax.

jewellcr and silversmith. McCulloch took considerable interest in civic affairs, serving as alderman and school commissioner, and was instrumental in establishing the popular Public Gardens.

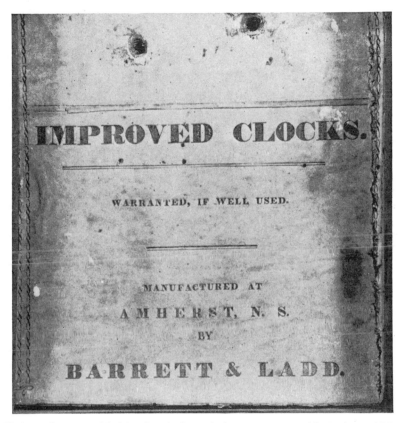

No. 43. Manufacturer's label in the clock made by Barrett & Ladd, Amherst, N.S.

One of McCulloch's apprentices was Thomas Charles Johnson (1853-1923), a native of Halifax who began business for himself about 1874 as a watchmaker. About 1891 his two sons, Charles E. and Albert G., were taken into the business, and the firm of T. C. Johnson and Sons continues at 441 Barrington Street as watchmakers, jewellers and importers.

# CHAPTER SIX

# Pianoforte Companies in Nova Scotia

Pianos were manufactured in Nova Scotia in the nineteenth century by several companies, such as H. & J. Philips, William Fraser and Sons, Williams and Leverman, Brockley and Company, the Gates' Organ and Piano Company, and Amherst Pianos, still commonly found in Cumberland County. A list of some piano companies in Nova Scotia may be found in Appendix E. The actions were imported from Chickerings', Steinway's, or Broadwood's, but all other work was done in the province.

Until the mid-nineteenth century pianos were a rarity, available only to the comparatively wealthy and lovingly cherished by their owners. Every district has traditions of its first spinet or piano, more often than not imported from England. When Lord Dalhousie was governor of Nova Scotia from 1816 to 1820, he imported a spinet from Broadwood's in London for Mary Ross, the daughter of his friend and fellow-officer, Captain William Ross. This spinet was taken by sailing ship from Halifax to Chester Basin, and was carried on the backs of soldiers about fifteen miles through the woods to New Ross in the interior of Lunenburg County. All the inhabitants of the county around came to see this exquisite instrument and to admire the beautiful mahogany case. This spinet is now on view at the Public Archives of Nova Scotia.

Henry J. Philips came to Halifax about 1845 from Hamburg in Germany with pianos to sell, and was so successful that he persuaded John H. Philips to join him. Together they formed the firm of H. & J. Philips, and began to manufacture pianofortes in Halifax. Sir John Harvey, the lieutenant-governor of Nova Scotia from 1846 to 1852, purchased their first instrument. Later it was claimed that the Philipses were "the first to produce a piano in the Province." As early as 1832, however, B. Slade was advertising in the *Nova Scotian* that he was an "Organ Builder and Piano Forte Maker" from England, and was asking for patronage, so a few pianos may have been made in Nova Scotia before the arrival of the Philipses.

In 1852 Messrs. George and William Moir were building pianofortes in Halifax in their establishment at the corner of Duke and Barrington Streets. In the same year H. J. Philips was exhorting people to "encourage Home Manufacture" by buying one of his 6½ octave piccolo pianofortes with double action, "warranted to stand the climate." In Cunnabell's Almanac for 1857 John B. Philips was advertising himself as the "Inventor and Manufacturer of the Iron Piano Forte." In 1858 he was being praised for the splendid concert grand piano he had built for the use of the Temperance Society, but a year later he sold his stock and goodwill and left the country.

On display in the Provincial Museum at Citadel Hill is an upright or cottage pianoforte made about 1850 by Henry J. Philips. The case is of rosewood, with a panel of red pleated silk, and has heavy six-sided legs. It originally belonged to Joseph R. Bennett, a West India merchant of Halifax. The maker's label is printed in gold on black glossy paper with a gilt border: "Henry J. Philips/Piano Forte Manufacturer/No. 121 Granville Street/Halifax, N.S." The total height of the piano is 63.50"; width of front, 47.40"; depth at key-board, 23.70"; depth of case for strings, 10.70". The frame for the strings is of wood; strings vertical, two strings to each note except in the five lowest bass notes; six and a half octaves, C to G inclusive.

The Philips' firm was purchased in August 1859 by William Fraser and Sons, and removed to 88 Barrington Street. William Fraser had been born in Aberdeen, Scotland, emigrating when nineteen years of age to Halifax, where he engaged in furniture making. At the Nova Scotian Exhibition of 1854 he won first prize for a walnut sofa, a mahogany centre table, half a dozen drawing-room chairs, and a walnut fire screen.

Fraser was manufacturing pianos in Halifax as early as 1856, and in later years his sons Thomas James and William Samuel were in the partnership. William, junior, invented what were known as Fraser's patent curved-end keys. The firm was still in business in 1890. Their pianos were exhibited at the London International Exhibition in 1862, when the commissioners reported that "the pianos sent by Messrs. Fraser & Sons, and by Messrs. Brockley, Misener & Co., were great additions to the [Nova Scotian] court."

William Fraser and Sons made a splendid instrument as an example of local piano manufacture for the Paris International Exhibition of 1867, at

No. 44. Upright rosewood piano manufactured at Halifax about 1850 by Henry J. Philips and now at the Provincial Museum, Citadel Hill, Halifax.

No. 45. Piano carved of bird's-eye maple at Halifax by William Fraser and Sons, and exhibited at the Paris International Exhibition of 1867.

which it received a special prize. The action was imported, but the case was constructed in Fraser's factory and the keys were Fraser's patent curved-end keys. The case was made of Nova Scotian bird's-eye maple skilfully executed in foliated design, backed by purple velvet. In the opinion of the late Harry Piers, it was carved by Henry Dewismes. Anyone who has worked with bird's-eye maple will realize what labour would be involved in the carving of a piano case from it. This instrument was presented to the Nova Scotia Museum of Science by Miss Mary Fraser of Halifax, a grand-daughter of the manufacturer, and may be seen at the Museum's Branch at Citadel Hill.

Another firm that first made furniture and later transferred its interest to pianos was Williams and Leverman. William Williams and Henry A. Leverman started business in Halifax about 1859 in the woodturning and jig-saw work. Their premises being burned in 1871, they constructed a new factory at 15-17 Carleton Street. There they were joined by William Leverman, who had learned the trade of piano making from H. & J. Philips and William Fraser.

In 1876 their factory occupied two large wooden buildings and employed twenty workmen. One structure contained lathes, saws and other machinery, all operated by an eight-horsepower steam engine. The other was used for manufacturing and polishing the cases, and setting up the pianos. All the parts of the instruments were manufactured locally except the keys and part of the action. Two hundred pianos had been made in five years. Native woods were used because they were better adapted to the climate than foreign woods.

Thomas Brockley had learned his trade with Broadwood's, the famous London pianoforte maufacturers, and for thirty years had been foreman in the firm of Broadwood and Stodard. In 1856 he was persuaded to come to Halifax to work with J. B. Philips, but the partnership did not materialize. Instead, Alfred W. Brockley came from London in 1857 to join his father, and John Misener, a local cabinetmaker, was associated with them until 1863.

Brockley and Company flourished and expanded. In 1876, the year they exhibited at the Philadelphia Centennial, they were manufacturing pianos in all styles, ranging in price from $200 to $1,000. They also sold cabinet organs. They had obtained honourable mention and £25 for a cottage piano exhibited at the London International Exhibition of 1862. "Their instruments are used with the highest satisfaction in Halifax and the Province, and they have found their way to far off Manitoba, the United States, the West Indies and even to England," according to an account of *Halifax and Its Business* in 1876.

A local organ builder was James Hepburn of Pictou, who won a certificate and a prize of £7 10s. for an organ suitable for a small church or hall at the Nova Scotian Exhibition of 1854. In 1860 James Hepburn built a pipe organ with 400 pipes for the Assembly Hall in Pictou. "Congregations should no longer look afield for organs, when such fine instruments can be manufactured here," proudly wrote the editor of the *Eastern Chronicle*.

John Bath Reed raised the frame of an organ factory at Bridgetown in 1881, and in September of that year a church organ had been completed for the Providence Methodist Church. A year later J. P. Rice and A. E. Sulis were running the factory for Reed, and the organ for the Baptist Church in Paradise was secured from them.

The Gates' Organ and Piano Company catered to the popularity of the reed organ as an elegant feature of the Victorian parlour. The three Gates brothers began making pianos and organs at Melvern Square, Annapolis County, about 1872. In their first year they produced only twenty-five instruments. In 1882, however, they reorganized their company with a capital of $60,000 in fifty-dollar shares, and removed to larger premises in Truro, a central railway junction, where they planned to employ fifty workmen producing eight hundred instruments a year. At the Colonial and Indian Exhibition at London in 1886 they displayed cabinet organs and wood for the inside work of pianos.

 CHAPTER SEVEN

# The Romance of Collecting Furniture

### EXHIBITIONS

By 1860 Nova Scotian craftsmen had reached such a point of excellence that they were proud to send some outstanding examples of their musical instruments and furniture which had been made from native woods to the International Exhibition which was held at London in 1862.

The commissioners for Nova Scotia reported that the "beautiful specimens of furniture contributed by Messrs. McEwan & Reid, and by Messrs. Gordon & Keith, and the pianos sent by Messrs. Fraser & Sons, and by Messrs. Brockley, Misener, & Co., were great additions to the [Nova Scotian] court, and proved that the people of the province could not only appreciate and enjoy, but could also produce those articles of luxury which are the evidence and the results of refinement and civilization. Very great surprise was expressed by visitors at these articles coming from Nova Scotia. . . ."

The severe competition that the furniture encountered was emphasized by the commissioners. Therefore they were highly gratified that the only medal in this class awarded to the contributions from North America was carried off by McEwan and Reid of Halifax for excellent workmanship in sofas, chairs, and a cabinet of native wood. The Halifax firm of Gordon and Keith received honourable mention for the high quality of their furniture. Nova Scotia received as large a proportion of awards as any department at the International Exhibition, as nineteen medals and eleven honourable mentions were won by sixty-five exhibitors.

96

The Nova Scotian commissioners pointed out that among the manufacturers listed in the census of 1861 were one hundred and forty-seven cabinetmakers, fifteen chairmakers, three chair and three cabinet factories, one woodenware factory and one pail factory. Joseph Howe said that when told "that Nova Scotia is behind other States in manufactures, we can point to our shipyards, every one of which is a manufactory furnishing healthy employment in the open air." The shipping owned in Nova Scotia in the year 1860 and employed in the fisheries and coasting trade amounted to 3,258 vessels, with a gross tonnage of 248,061 tons, being almost a ton for every man, woman and child in the province.

At the Paris Exposition of 1867 the space allotted to Nova Scotia was limited. The only furniture exhibited was a piano by W. Fraser and Son, a school desk and chair by Currie, fancy chairs with India-work seats by G. Newcomb, and a cabinet made of native wood by McEwan and Son.

### IMPORTED FURNITURE

Furniture made in Nova Scotia always had to meet competition from furnishings brought into the province by military and naval personnel. For over one hundred and fifty years Halifax continued as a base for Imperial power, and visitors from England commented on the striking similarity of the city in appearance and social life to a small garrison town in England. Until Confederation there were usually three British regiments stationed at Halifax, and in time of war there might be as many as seven. In 1870 the Imperial troops were withdrawn from the rest of Canada and the headquarters of the commander-in-chief transferred to Halifax where two Imperial regiments were stationed. The regiments usually remained in garrison for three years' service.

Halifax was also the naval base of the Atlantic Squadron from May to October, and the number of ships on the North American and West Indian station varied from ten to twenty.

In the days when a gentleman still had to purchase his commission in the armed services, the officers stationed at Halifax were men of wealth, and often belonged to the nobility. They imported expensive furniture into the province, and often sold it when transferred to another post. Thus prosperous merchants were able to buy handsome English furniture at the military auctions.

Prince Edward, later Duke of Kent and father of Queen Victoria, commanded the British garrison in Nova Scotia from 1794 to 1800. When His Royal Highness was promoted in 1799 to be commander-in-chief of the forces in British North America, he ordered from England new equipment suitable to his rank of lieutenant-general. Furniture, wines, a library and map collection, carriages and horses and livestock valued in all at £11,000 were shipped from Portsmouth on the *Francis*. On December 22, 1799, the ship was driven by a southeast gale on the sands of Sable Island and all on board were lost— including Prince Edward's personal surgeon and family, his coachman and four stableboys.

Despite such difficulties, the Duke of Kent succeeded in furnishing his Town House on the glacis of Citadel Hill, and his summer residence at Prince's Lodge five miles from Halifax. Harry Piers, late curator of the Provincial Museum of Nova Scotia, claimed that the furnishings of the Duke of Kent's Town House were sold by auction when the Duke left Halifax in 1800, but that those in Prince's Lodge became the property of Sir John Wentworth. Various articles that once belonged to the Duke of Kent are cherished by Nova Scotians. With the exception of the Windsor chair used by the Duke in the Theatre Royal and later presented to St. Andrew's Masonic Lodge in Halifax, furnishings belonging to the Duke are made of mahogany. Two mahogany chairs belonging to the Duke of Kent may be seen at Uniacke House at Mount Uniacke, Hants County.

The source of much present-day antique furniture may be traced to auctions held in Halifax by service personnel, both navy and army. On June 25, 1817, Moody and Boyle held an auction at the North Barracks of household furniture of John Beckwith, who was returning to England. This Nova Scotian had fought in Spain with the Duke of Wellington and had lost a leg at Waterloo. Colonel Duke's auction in 1818 included everything that a person of rank would need in a colonial outpost such as furniture, three horses, tilbury gig, saddles, bridles, madeira wine, champagne, an excellent fowling piece, J. Manton pistols, books, maps and telescopes. "The tables and much other of the FURNITURE were made by Morgan & Sanders, London."

Morgan and Sanders were upholsterers and cabinetmakers at "Trafalgar House," Nos. 16 and 17, Catherine Street, three doors from the Strand, London, from 1803 to 1817. They specialized in army and navy equipage, took out various patents for extending dining tables and "adaptable" four-post bedsteads, and had a table that could be extended to dine twenty persons and could be packed in a bar ten inches deep.

Examples of furniture imported for gentlemen's homes in Nova Scotia in the nineteenth century may be seen at Clifton in Windsor and Uniacke House at Mount Uniacke. Clifton was built from 1833 to 1836 by Judge Thomas C. Haliburton. Uniacke House was constructed in 1813-1815 for Attorney-General Richard John Uniacke, and remained the home of the Uniacke family for over a century. Both houses are now owned by the province of Nova Scotia and are open to the public during the summer season.

### FOREIGN COMPETITION

About 1826 the importation of American furniture was affecting the trade of local cabinetmakers to such an extent that they appealed to the House of Assembly for an additional duty on foreign importations. They explained that "a large quantity of furniture, such as has been usually manufactured for sale by your Petitioners, has been imported from Boston and disposed of at public auction . . . That cabinetmakers in the great towns of the United States are enabled to make furniture at lower prices than will remunerate your Petitioners, because the trade there is carried on upon a larger scale. . . . That mahogany in particular can be bought in Boston or New York often at one half what is asked for it in Halifax . . . your Petitioners apprehend that furniture will be sent here by speculators and insolvent persons and sold at an under value, and in this manner injure the mechanics who reside here and contribute to the support of Government by the payment of taxes and otherwise."

These twenty-four cabinetmakers said that furniture was protected by only fifteen per cent duty, and "it appears to them to be an unwise and mistaken policy to encourage the industry of foreigners, by laying open this market to them, without securing to the resident tradesmen a sufficient preference. . . . "

No. 46. Signatures of Nova Scotian cabinetmakers petitioning the House of Assembly in 1826 for an additional duty on foreign furniture. COURTESY OF PUBLIC ARCHIVES OF NOVA SCOTIA.

Dr. Abraham Gesner in *The Industrial Resources of Nova Scotia,* which was published in 1849, noted that this competition was continuing in the mid-nineteenth century.

It may be admitted that the productions of the different tradesmen are well and substantially made; yet they ordinarily lack lightness, finish, and the ingenuity peculiar to articles manufactured in the United States, to which a great many of our best mechanics emigrate annually. Numbers of waggons, and other kinds of carriages, farming utensils, wooden clocks, and household furniture of every description, are annually imported from Boston, and other American ports. They at once recommend themselves, and are purchased at high prices, in preference to any made by the mechanics of the country.

Boston was sometimes referred to as the second capital of Nova Scotia as it was one of the earliest ports to which our ships traded, taking our mineral production, such as coal and gypsum, and bringing back manufactured goods. With the completion of the Intercolonial Railway to Quebec and Ontario in 1876, competition from these areas put a further strain on local production in the Maritimes. The closing of the Cumming furniture factory at New Glasgow is an example of the fate that overtook so many small Nova Scotian industries when high tariffs made it difficult to continue to do business with Great Britain and the United States, and forced them to turn their trade channels via the railway.

### THE EXODUS

The great depressions of the 1870's and 1880's gave marked impetus to the exodus of Nova Scotians to New England and other parts of the United States, and to Ontario, the Prairie Provinces and British Columbia as the economy of the area could no longer support its natural increase in population. Although the population of Nova Scotia has increased from 387,800 at the time of Confederation to 694,717 in 1956, the percentage of Canada's people living in the province has fallen from 10% to 5%.

Many of those who left were young men or women in search of a fortune, but others were families who took cherished heirlooms with them.

**Office of PAINE'S NEW FURNITURE MANUFACTORY.**

*Nos. 141, 143, 145, 147, 149, 151, 153 & 155 Friend Street.*
*48, 50, 52, 54, 56, 58, 60 & 62 Canal Street.*
*10, 12 & 14 Market Street.*

Boston, Augt 29 1876

Mr D. Logan  Picton N.S.

**Bought of J. S. Paine**

IMPORTER AND MANUFACTURER OF

**FASHIONABLE FURNITURE.**

Goods received at Elevator A & B.    Delivered at 14 Market St.

Extension Tables, Dining, Office, Easy, Folding and Step Ladder Chairs, Parlor Suits, Sofas, Divans, Tete, Piano Stools. Pine, Chestnut, Ash, Black Walnut, Rosewood and Mahogany Chamber Suits. Centre and Inlaid Tables; Office and Parlor Desks; Book-Cases, Wardrobes, Etageres, Mattress, Church and School Furniture, Bedsteads, Spring Beds, Window Drapery, Mantle, Parlor and Mirror Ornaments, Umbrella Stands, Bouquet Stands, Fancy Brackets, Furniture Castors. Furniture Polish, Mattresses and Bedding, Blankets, Comforters, Sheets and Pillow Cases, Feathers, Curled Hair, Husks and Excelsior, Cloths, Carpets, Stoves and Crockery.

COST OF PACKING TO BE ADDED TO THIS BILL
Goods sold for Cash, only conditionally delivered until paid for.

ALL GOODS SOLD FOR CASH ARE SOLD AND DELIVERED UPON THE EXPRESS CONDITION, THAT THE PROPERTY THEREIN SHALL NOT VEST IN THE PURCHASER, UNTIL THE SAME ARE PAID FOR.

| | | | | |
|---|---|---|---|---|
| 1 | Champion Parlor Suite Gray Hair Cloth | | 90 00 | |
| 1 | Ash B. W. Trimmed #10 Marble Top Set | | 65 00 | |
| 1 | Pine Set | | 25 00 | |
| 1 | Wood Top Centre Table | | 8 00 | |
| 1 | #3 H. C. Lounge | | 14 00 | |
| 6 | Stained B. A. Dining | 170 | 10 20 | |
| 1 | 10ft Ash Exten Table | | 11 00 | |
| 1 | 32 x 18 Mantle Mirror | | 11 50 | |
| 1 | Guy H. C Ottoman Red Top | | 6 00 | |
| 1 | Small H. Top Boquet Stand | | 4 00 | |
| 1 | Tucker Spring | | 4 00 | |
| 1 | Fibre Mattress | | 7 00 | 255 70 |
| 85 | Yards Mats | 12½ | 10 63 | |
| 50 | Lbs. Excelsior | 2½ | 1 25 | |
| 1 | Marble Box | | 1 00 | |
| 1 | Glass " | | 2 00 | 14 88 |
| | | | | 270 58 |

No. 47.  Bill of sale from Paine's furniture factory.  In the possession of the author.

Still more Nova Scotian furniture has left the province as it has been inherited by a son in Ontario, a grandson in Saskatchewan, a daughter in Massachusetts, or a great-niece in California. In Montreal there is a secretary-bookcase made by A. Morton of Halifax taken there by an elderly Nova Scotian clergyman. Indeed, Nova Scotian furniture has been carried all over the world by the sons and daughters of our province. Our furniture has also been sold abroad; after the International Exhibition of 1862, for example, furniture and other articles were sold in London, and recently articles of Nova Scotian manufacture were auctioned in the English capital. Most of the Cumming furniture was sold in the United States, although some stayed in Pictou County, where it still turns up as one by one the old families and old homes sell off their inherited pieces by auction. Other furniture made locally has been shipped away by antique dealers. We have had prime examples of English craftsmanship imported to Nova Scotia, as auction notices in Halifax newspapers have shown. The collections that exist in Nova Scotia today are the remains of these auctions and later importations from England and the United States.

Nova Scotia has been mined for furniture for the past sixty years, some of this being sold south of the border as made in New England. Depressions and Scottish thrift have made Nova Scotians keep the furniture of their forefathers, however, and brides and grooms have bought it at farm auctions as old families have died out. Our coal mines may be economically uncertain, yet the Nova Scotian antique market is apparently inexhaustible and many pieces are now being exported to Ontario. Recently an antique dealer purchased twelve-hundred spinning wheels in Cape Breton while holidaying there.

### CRAFTSMEN

Until recently there have been craftsmen capable of duplicating the many fine pieces of furniture that have stood the test of time and favour. The writer remembers his grandfather, George McLaren of Pictou, a third generation cabinetmaker, making furniture in 1920 to order for Pictou County homes. The furniture consisted mainly of dining tables of walnut, ash or elm, selling for $12, and of bedroom furniture stained and grained to imitate mahogany.

About this time the last of the old craftsmen were giving way to the machine age, leaving behind many fine examples of their work. At present Eric Bagnald of Bedford, Halifax County, is carrying on furniture making in the old tradition of fine quality workmanship.

No. 48. George McLaren's advertisement, Pictou, N.S., 1885.

### THE ROMANCE OF COLLECTING

Growing up in a family closely allied with cabinetmaking and with the collecting and selling of antiques, I was able to observe the disposal of many well-furnished homes and the trials and joys of furniture collecting. After minor repairs and repolishings these antiques were then sold across Canada and the United States until one finds that wherever one travels today some town or city has furniture that originated in Nova Scotia. The classic example of furniture-travel, I think, is a mahogany drum table that was made in Halifax about 1810 by Tulles, Pallister and M'Donald, and then turned up in England in 1956 when it was purchased by an Englishman and taken to Peru.

One comes across many amusing incidents during the collecting and selling of antiques. I well remember my father buying a genuine Sheraton sideboard that he found in the back room of a Pictou County butcher shop. As the top had a substantial mahogany board it had been used to cut meat! During the years the top became badly marked from the knives and cleavers, but my father was able to reverse the top board.

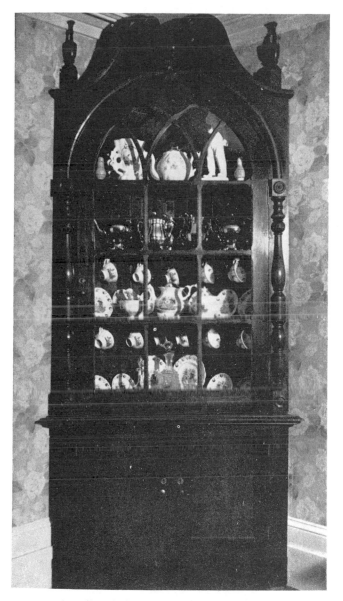

No. 49. Mahogany corner cupboard made by George McLaren about 1900. Now in the possession of Mrs. F. MacKenzie of Pictou, N.S.

A lady fell in love with the Sheraton sideboard and took it home in triumph. A few weeks later she returned in tears because some friends had made fun of her for buying an old stand the butcher had used and she had been humiliated. With another buyer willing to take it off her hands at a profit of one hundred dollars my father offered to make arrangements for its resale. With tears in her eyes she said: "Butcher shop or not, I'll never sell. I love it."

Another incident concerned a grandfather clock that had been thrown down the stairs during a family quarrel. My father purchased the remains and repaired it. Today the clock is ticking away somewhere in Florida, but it will take a hurricane to stop it again.

Mrs. F. B. Payzant has described how one warm summer afternoon she stopped in a village to ask about antique furniture in the neighbourhood. One man told her to go to a certain house about half a mile away that he pointed out saying: "You'll find an interesting antique there, all right."

In the heat she crossed a rough field, but the only antique in the house was a glaring old woman—the mother-in-law of the practical joker. Hot and cross as the furniture collector was, she inwardly acknowledged the joke but returned to the car by another path to avoid meeting the joker.

Another day, halting at a farmhouse, Mrs. Payzant spied the knobs of a chair through the window and immediately recognized a Sibley. Fortunately the owner had several and was as glad to sell as the lady was to purchase, so the chair was brought home in the trunk of the car. On another occasion Mrs. Payzant was filled with joy when she was triumphantly able to prove to an antique collector that some beautiful pieces of old furniture that were considered to be of English origin had really been made in Nova Scotia.

Never have the collecting activities of Nova Scotia been greater than during the past decade. Families with old furniture are beginning to cherish it as they have long cherished family portraits. Younger people are collecting antiques both for their beauty and as investments that are likely to increase in value over the years. It is becoming steadily more difficult to discover handmade furniture than can be bought for next to nothing.

A broadening of outlook is partly responsible for this urge to collect. In earlier years most collecting was done by sea captains who brought back from the far corners of the globe curios ranging from sharks' teeth to ivory boxes. Today travel for pleasure and moves in search of employment have quickened interest in the treasures of other regions and countries, and a further result has been a quest for what remains of Nova Scotia's own past.

The worth of pioneer craftsmanship has been established by the test of time. Shoddy and cheap furniture soon falls to pieces; only the good remains. In this age of machine production more and more people are learning to appreciate the artistry of early cabinetmakers and chairmakers who created beautiful pieces of furniture for us to admire and use.

# Key to the Appendices

26  *Acadian Recorder* for 1823.

27  *Acadian Recorder* for 1824.

28  *Acadian Recorder* for 1826.

29  House of Assembly of Nova Scotia: Petitions on Trade and Industry—protest from local cabinetmakers in 1826.

30  *Nova Scotian* for 1827.

31  *Nova Scotian* for 1828.

32  *Nova Scotian* for 1829.

33  *Acadian Recorder* for 1831.

34  *Pictou Observer* for 1831.

35  *Pictou Bee* for 1835.

36  *Mechanic & Farmer*, Pictou, 1839.

37  *Eastern Chronicle*, Pictou, 1841.

38  *Eastern Chronicle* for 1842.

39  *Morning Post*, Halifax, 1843.

40  *Eastern Chronicle*, Pictou, 1847.

41  *Eastern Chronicle* for 1848.

42  *Halifax Sun*, 1849.

43  Census of Nova Scotia for 1860-61 (20 volumes)

44  Pictou County Cemetery Lists compiled by Henry C. Ritchie.

45A Nugent's Business Directory of City of Halifax for 1858-59.

45  *The Halifax Business Directory* for 1863 . . . compiled and published by Luke Hutchinson.

46  Hutchinson's *Nova Scotia Directory* for 1864-65.

47  Hutchinson's *Nova Scotia Directory* for 1866-67.

48  McAlpine's *Maritime Provinces Directory*, 1870-71.

49  McAlpine's *Nova Scotia Directory* for 1868-69.

50  McAlpine's *Halifax City Directory* for 1869-70.

51  McAlpine's *Halifax City Directory* for 1870-71.

52  McAlpine's *Halifax City Directory* for 1871-72.

53  McAlpine's *Halifax City Directory* for 1873-74.

54  McAlpine's *Halifax City Directory* for 1875-76.

55  McAlpine's *Halifax City Director* for 1876-77.

56  McAlpine's *Halifax City Directory* for 1877-78.

57  McAlpine's *Halifax City Directory* for 1878-79.

58  McAlpine's *Halifax City Directory* for 1880-81.

59  McAlpine's *Halifax City Directory* for 1881-82.

60 McAlpine's *Halifax City Directory* for 1882-83.

61 McAlpine's *Halifax City Directory* for 1883-84.

62 McAlpine's *Halifax City Directory* for 1884-85.

63 McAlpine's *Halifax City Directory* for 1885-86.

64 McAlpine's *Halifax City Directory* for 1886-87.

65 McAlpine's *Halifax City Directory* for 1887-88.

66 McAlpine's *Halifax City Directory* for 1888-89.

67 McAlpine's *Halifax City Directory* for 1889-90.

68 McAlpine's *Nova Scotia Directory* for 1890-97.

69 Teare's *Directory of Pictou and New Glasgow* for 1879-80.

70 *Morning Herald* (Halifax, N.S.) August 22, 1887, p. 3 has a list of those working for Gordon and Keith when their furniture factory was destroyed by fire.

71 *Morning Herald,* January 1, 1886 supplement to New Year's Edition.

72 MARRIAGE BONDS for the Province of Nova Scotia for 1813-15.

73 MARRIAGE BONDS for the Province of Nova Scotia for 1833.

74 Piers, Harry & Mackay, Donald C., *Master Goldsmiths and Silversmiths of Nova Scotia and Their Marks.*

75 Belcher's Farmers' Almanacs.

76 Cameron, James M.—*Industrial History of New Glasgow* (Hector Publishing Co., New Glasgow, N.S., 1960)

There are more cabinetmakers in Halifax, partly because Halifax was the largest centre of population in the province, and partly because more directories have been published for this city. Many of the cabinetmakers and chairmakers in the rural districts carried on their craft much longer than the dates indicate, but lack of records make it impossible to tell how long they did remain. The Census of 1860-61, and some of the earlier censuses, do not show occupation.

# APPENDIX A

*An alphabetical list of cabinetmakers in Nova Scotia.*

Where a dash appears before a date (—1826) it means that the cabinetmaker was working before this date, but I have not been able to ascertain for how long. A dash after a date (1860—) means that the cabinetmaker continued in business after this date.

| Name | Address | Dates in Business | Reference No. |
|------|---------|-------------------|---------------|
| ADAMS, THOMAS | Halifax, Halifax Co. | 1815 | (72) |

On December 19, 1815 he took out a marriage bond to marry Jane Williamson.

| | | | |
|------|---------|-------------------|---------------|
| ADAMSON, JAMES | Pictou, Pictou Co. | 1838 | (15) |
| ALEXANDER, CHARLES | Halifax, Halifax Co. | —1826-1827 | (29, 30) |

Hollis Street.
Cabinetmaker, upholsterer, and undertaker. The co-partnership between Alexander and Thomson was dissolved September 16, 1826.

| | | | |
|------|---------|-------------------|---------------|
| ALEXANDER, GEORGE | Halifax, Halifax Co. | 1820 | |

On July 21, 1820 he took out a marriage bond to marry Mary Killikor.

| | | | |
|------|---------|-------------------|---------------|
| ALLEN, CHARLES P. | Halifax, Fall River and Waverley in Halifax Co. | 1831-1862 | (14, 17, 33) |

Chairmaker, he had a factory at Fall River and a warehouse on Bauer's Wharf in Halifax City, later built home in Waverley. He became a British citizen in 1848.

| | | | |
|------|---------|-------------------|---------------|
| ALLISON, PENDERMAN | Windsor, Hants Co. | 1791 | (9) |
| | Falmouth, Hants Co. | 1791-1795 | (9) |
| ANDERSON, R. J. | Halifax, Halifax Co. | 1890-1897 | (68) |

Foreman for Halifax Furniture Company.

| | | | |
|------|---------|-------------------|---------------|
| ANDERSON, WILLIAM G. | Halifax, Halifax Co. | 1826-1865 | (14, 29) |
| ANDERSON, WILLIAM G., JR. | Halifax, Halifax Co. | 1864-1865 | (46) |
| ANDERSON & MALCOM | Halifax, Halifax Co. | 1827-1828 | (30) |

Cabinetmakers, joiners, upholsterers, undertakers.
James Malcom

| | | | |
|------|---------|-------------------|---------------|
| ARENBURG, JAMES | Lunenburg, Lunenburg Co. | 1890-1897 | (68) |
| ASHMORE, GEORGE | Halifax, Halifax Co. | 1864-1869 | (46, 47, 49) |
| ASHMORE, HENRY | Halifax, Halifax Co. | 1864-1865 | (46) |
| BAGNALD, E. H. | Sackville, Halifax Co. | —1950 to present | |
| BALL, PETER | Township of Guysborough, and Manchester, Guysborough Co. | 1792 | (10) |
| BARBER, JOHN | Halifax, Halifax Co. | 1826 | (29) |
| BARNES, JAMES | Halifax, Halifax Co. | 1838 | (14) |

| | | | |
|---|---|---|---|
| BARRETT, A. W. | Wallace, Cumberland Co. | 1868-1869 | (49) |
| BARRETT, F. | Halifax, Halifax Co. | 1887 | (70) |

Cabinetmaker at Gordon & Keith.

| | | | |
|---|---|---|---|
| BAXTER, JAMES | Halifax, Halifax Co. | 1864-1870 | (46, 47, 49, 50) |
| 18 Prince St. | | | |

| | | | |
|---|---|---|---|
| BAXTER, JOHN | Halifax, Halifax Co. | —1832-1838— | (14, 35) |

On August 9, 1832, he advertised that John Gordon, a carpenter in his employ, had stolen £7 from him.

| | | | |
|---|---|---|---|
| BAXTER, ROBERT | Halifax, Halifax Co. | 1869-1870 | (50) |
| 18 Prince St. | | 1882-1885 | (60-62) |
| BAXTER BROS. | Halifax, Halifax Co. | 1871-1881 | (52-58) |
| 18 Prince St. | | | |
| Richard Baxter. | | | |
| Robert Baxter. | | | |

| | | | |
|---|---|---|---|
| BEATTIE, EBENEZER | Londonderry Township, Colchester Co. | 1838 | (15) |

| | | | |
|---|---|---|---|
| BENNETT, A. | Wallace, Cumberland Co. | 1864-1869 | (46, 47, 49) |
| BENNETT, WILLIAM | Halifax, Halifax Co. | 1876-1877 | (55) |
| BENT, JOHN Z. | Bridgetown, Annapolis Co. | 1890-1897 | (68) |
| BIGBY, JAMES J. | Halifax, Halifax Co. | 1864-1879 | (46, 47, 49, 57) |

Cabinetmaker and undertaker.
    36 Gerrish St. (1866-67)
      Gerrish n. Gottingen (1868-69)
      84 Gerrish St. (1869-72)
      83 Gerrish St. (1873-79)

| | | |
|---|---|---|
| Elizabeth, widow of James, boards 9 Morris St. (1878-79) | | (57) |

| | | | |
|---|---|---|---|
| BIGELOW, BENJAMIN | River Philip, Cumberland Co. | 1864-1865 | (46) |
| BISHOP, SILAS | Morristown, Kings Co. | 1864-1869 | (46, 47, 48) |

Cabinet factory and wool carder.

| | | | |
|---|---|---|---|
| BLACK, JAMES | Halifax, Halifax Co. | 1864-1869 | (46, 47, 49) |
| 179 Albemarle St. (1866-67) | | | |
| 123 Barrack St. (1868-69) | | | |

| | | | |
|---|---|---|---|
| BLACK, WM. | Shelburne, Shelburne Co. | 1786-1787 | (8) |
| St. John's St. | | | |

| | | | |
|---|---|---|---|
| BLACKADAR, WM. C. | Wolfville, Kings Co. | 1864-1869 | (46, 48) |
| BOND, JOHN | Halifax, Halifax Co. | 1792-1793 | (9, 11) |
| Chairmaker. | | | |

| | | | |
|---|---|---|---|
| BOREHAM, W. R. | Halifax, Halifax Co. | 1873-1874 | (53) |
| 85 Argyle St. | | | |

| | | | |
|---|---|---|---|
| BOUTILIER, G. E. W. | Bedford, Halifax Co. | —1955— | (46) |
| BRADY, ROBERT | Petite Riviere, Lun. Co. | 1864-1869 | (46, 48) |
| BRADY, THOMAS | Halifax, Halifax Co. | 1838 | (14) |

| | | | |
|---|---|---|---|
| BRANDER, JOHN<br>(Older brother of Robert Brander)<br>    161-165 Barrington St. (1863-72)<br>    185 Barrington St. (1873-74)<br>    181 Granville St. (1876-81) | Halifax, Halifax Co. | —1831, 1838<br>1863-1881 | (14, 33)<br>(45, 47, 49-58,<br>67-68) |
| BRANDER, JOHN C.<br>(Son of Robert Brander, q.v.)<br>    161-165 Barrington St. (1866-69)<br>    34 Sackville St. (1890-97) | Halifax, Halifax Co. | 1864-1869 | (47-49, 50, 68) |
| BRANDER, ROBERT (1832-1909.<br>From Huntley, Scotland.)<br>    58 Barrington St. (1863-67)<br>    27 Sackville St. (1868-72)<br>    34 Sackville St. (1873-97)<br>He also made ships' wheels. | Halifax, Halifax Co. | 1857-1897 | (45, 47, 49, 68) |
| BRANDER, THOMAS | Halifax, Halifax Co. | 1868-1869 | (49) |
| BRANDER, WILLIAM R.<br>    18 Barrington St.<br>Upholsterer. | Halifax, Halifax Co. | 1890-1897 | (68) |
| BROWN, EDWARD | Paradise, Annapolis Co. | 1864-1865 | (46) |
| BROWN, HARRY U. | Halifax, Halifax Co. | 1864-1865 | (46) |
| BROWN, N.<br>A cabinetmaker at Gordon & Keith's factory. | Halifax, Halifax Co. | 1887 | (70) |
| BROWN, ROBERT | Truro, Colchester Co. | 1864-1865 | (46) |
| BRUSH, ALFRED | Halifax, Halifax Co. | 1868-1869 | (49) |
| BRUSH, JAMES<br>    48 Buckingham St. (1871-72)<br>    45 Buckingham St. (1873-74) | Halifax, Halifax Co. | 1864-1874 | (46, 47, 52, 53) |
| BRYMER, LUDLOW | Halifax, Halifax Co. | 1864-1865 | (46) |
| BURRIS, MATTHEW | Upper Musquodoboit,<br>Halifax Co. | 1838 | (14) |
| BUSHELL, THOMAS | Halifax, Halifax Co. | 1864-1867 | (46, 47) |
| CALLANDER, WILLIAM<br>    "Cabinet makers' & builders' work respectfully solicited."<br>    "Ship Carving Always on Hand."<br>    55 Barrington St. | Halifax, Halifax Co. | 1866-1867 | (47) |
| CARTER, WM. | Halifax, Halifax Co. | 1864-1865 | (46) |
| CHAFFIN, SAMUEL | Truro, Colchester Co. | 1890-1897 | (68) |
| CHURCHILL, ALBERT | Mill Village, Queens Co. | 1866-1867 | (47) |
| CLANCY, WM. | Halifax, Halifax Co. | 1864-1865 | (46) |
| CLARK, H.<br>    "from Boston. Mahogany chairs, chests and sofas." | Pictou, Pictou Co. | 1839 | (36) |

CLARK, HENRY                    Truro, Colchester Co.              1864-1869        (46, 49)

CLARK, RUFUS                    Waterville, Kings Co.             1864-1869        (46, 48)

CLAY, E.                        Halifax, Halifax Co.              1887             (70)
    A cabinetmaker at Gordon & Keith's factory.

CLEMENTS, CHARLES               Halifax, Halifax Co.              1887             (70)
    A cabinetmaker at Gordon & Keith's factory.

CLEMENTS, T.                    Halifax, Halifax Co.              1887             (70)
    A cabinetmaker at Gordon & Keith's factory.

COLE, GEORGE                    Rawdon Township, Hants Co. —1832-1859             (15)
    Chairmaker.

COLE, J.                        Rawdon Township, Hants Co. —1817-1827—            (12)
    Chairmaker.

COOK, GEORGE                    Halifax, Halifax Co.              1864-1867        (46-47)

COOMBES, W. & J.                Sackville & Barrington St.,       1858-1859        (45A)
                                Halifax.

COOMBES, WILLIAM                Halifax, Halifax Co.              1858-1887—       (45A, 46-47,
    In 1887 he was foreman at Gordon & Keith's furniture factory, and                    70)
had been employed there for 25 years.

CONNOR, DAVID                   West River, Pictou Co.            1864-1865        (46)

CONNORS, THOMAS                 Halifax, Halifax Co.              1887             (70)
    A cabinetmaker at Gordon & Keith's factory; in 1897 he is listed as a    (68)
wood carver there.

COSGROVE, PATRICK               Oxford, Cumberland Co.            1890-1897        (68)

COBEY & COOLAN
    (See COVEY & COOLAN)

COVEY & COOLAN                  Halifax, Halifax Co.              1876-1881        (55-58)
    160 Argyle St.
Thomas Covey.
James Coolan.

COWLING, GEORGE                 Halifax, Halifax Co.              1813-1826        (29, 72)
    On November 26, 1813, he took out a marriage bond to marry Catharine
Henley, spinster.

CREAM, M.                       Halifax, Halifax Co.              —1887—           (70)
    A cabinetmaker at Gordon & Keith's factory.

CREED, SAMUEL                   Halifax, Halifax Co.              1826-1831        (29, 33)
    99 Granville St., in the shop "lately occupied by Mr. F. Charman."
"Cabinet Maker, Upholdster (sic), and Undertaker."

CROLL, DAVID                    Halifax, Halifax Co.              1838             (14)

CUMMING, ANDREW                 Halifax, Halifax Co.              1792-1794        (9, 11)
    Had a shop in Granville St., according to the *Weekly Chronicle* of
September 13, 1794.

CUMMING BROS.      New Glasgow, Pictou Co.    1879-1897    (68-69)
    Duncan Cumming.
    John Cumming.
    "Every description of Furniture, including sofa lounges, bureaus, chairs,
    bedsteads . . .'"

CUMMINGS, J.      Halifax, Halifax Co.    1815    (24)

CUMMINGS, JOHN      Piedmont Valley, Pictou Co.    1864-1867    (46, 47)
      New Glasgow, Pictou Co.    1868-1900    (45A, 76)

CUMMINGS, THOMAS      Halifax, Halifax Co.    1858-1884    (45, 45A, 47,
    173 Hollis St. (1858-59)                             49-50, 53-61)
    113 Hollis St. (1863)
     12 Prince St. (1866-69)
     43 Brunswick St. (1869-70)
    307 Brunswick St. (1873-78)
    212 Brunswick St. (1878-79)
    289 Brunswick St. (1880-84)
    In 1871-72 he is listed as foreman shipwright at H.M. Dockyard.

CUMMINGS, WILLIAM      Piedmont Valley, Pictou Co.    1864-1867    (46-47)

CURRAN, J.      Halifax, Halifax Co.    1887    (70)
    A cabinetmaker at Gordon & Keith's factory.

CURRIE & HOWARD      Amherst, Cumberland Co.    1890-1897    (68)
    John M. Currie.
    James K. Howard.
    Manufacturers and dealers in Furniture.

CURRY, EDWARD      Windsor, Hants Co.    1864-1869    (46, 49)
    Wheelwright and cabinetmaker on King Street.
    "manufacturer of Patent Desks & Chairs &c for Schools, also Chamber
    Setts, Bureaus, Sinks, Wash Stands, Toilet Tables, Bedsteads, Leaf
    Tables, Chairs, Lounges etc."

CURRY, ELISHA      Windsor, Hants Co.    1870

DALLING, WM.      Halifax, Halifax Co.    1864-1865    (46)

DANE, JAMES B.      Yarmouth, Yarmouth Co.    1864-1865    (46)

DANIELS, PETER      Conquerall, Lunenburg Co.    1864-1869    (46, 49)

DAUPHINEE, ALBERT      Halifax, Halifax Co.    1884    (62)

DECOURSEY, A. B.      Halifax, Halifax Co.    1878-1879    (57)
    18 Barrington St.

DE FORREST, F.      Halifax, Halifax Co.    1864-1865    (46)

DE FREYTAS, JAMES      Halifax, Halifax Co.    1864-1869    (46, 49)

DEVINE, JOHN      Halifax, Halifax Co.    1858-1874    (45A, 45-47,
    68 Albemarle St.                                   53)

DEWER, ROBERT      Barney's River, Pictou Co.    1880

DIDHAM, J.      Halifax, Halifax Co.    1887    (70)
    A cabinetmaker in Gordon & Keith's factory.

| | | | |
|---|---|---|---|
| DILLON, THOMAS | Halifax, Halifax Co. | 1864-65 | (46) |
| DIXON, GEORGE M. | Oxford, Cumberland Co. | 1890-1897 | (68) |
| DOCKERILL, EDWARD | Halifax, Halifax Co. | 1864-1890 | (46-47, 62-67) |

In 1866-67 he is listed as a furniture polisher, and in 1890 as an upholsterer.

| | | | |
|---|---|---|---|
| DODGE, EDWIN C. | Digby, Digby Co. | 1864-1869 | (46, 47, 49) |
| DONOHUE, CHARLES | Halifax, Halifax Co. | 1884 | (62) |
| DOULL, G. M. | Amherst, Cumberland Co. | 1890-1897 | (68) |

Foreman of cabinet shop of Rhodes, Curry & Co.

| | | | |
|---|---|---|---|
| DOW, A. & SON | Halifax, Halifax Co. | 1864-1874 | (46-47, 49-53) |

Dow, Alexander.
Dow, Alexander, Jr.
In 1866-67 they were advertising as cabinetmakers and upholsterers at No. 19 Barrington Street—"Undertaking promptly attended to" and "Venetian Blinds Made to Order."

| | | | |
|---|---|---|---|
| DOW, ALEXANDER | Halifax, Halifax Co. | 1878-1881 | (57-58) |

118 Creighton St.

| | | | |
|---|---|---|---|
| DOW, ALEXANDER G. | Halifax, Halifax Co. | 1864 | (46) |
| DRAKE, JOHN | Dartmouth, Halifax Co. | 1864-1869 | (46-47, 49) |

Portland St.

| | | | |
|---|---|---|---|
| DRAPER, EDWARD | Halifax, Halifax Co. | —1749— | (1) |

Came from England with Governor Cornwallis' settlers.

| | | | |
|---|---|---|---|
| DRILLIO, ANDREW | Halifax, Halifax Co. | 1864-1869 | (46-47, 49) |
| DUNHAM, C. F. | Digby, Digby Co. | 1890-1897 | (68) |
| ELLIOTT, WILLIAM | Stillwater, Guysborough Co. | 1864-1867 | (46, 47) |

Cabinetmaker and carriagemaker.

| | | | |
|---|---|---|---|
| ELLIS, ABIJAH | Cedar Lake, Digby Co. | 1864-1869 | (46-49) |
| EMSLIE, JOHN | Bridgetown, Lawrencetown, and | 1833-1897 | (46, 47, 49, 68) |
| | Wilmot in Annapolis Co. | | |

At the N.S. Industrial Exhibition in October 1854 Emslie and Calnek of Bridgetown were awarded a prize of £10 for picture frames showing 58 specimens of native woods. John Emslie listed in Wilmot in 1866-67; in Lawrencetown in 1868-69, and at Bridgetown in directory for 1890-97.

| | | | |
|---|---|---|---|
| ESSON, GEORGE | | | |

(see THOMSON, JAMES)

| | | | |
|---|---|---|---|
| ESTANO, ROBERT | Halifax, Halifax Co. | 1864-1887 | (46, 47, 70) |

A cabinetmaker in Gordon & Keith's factory in 1887.

| | | | |
|---|---|---|---|
| EUREKA MANUFACTURING CO. LTD. | Oxford, Cumberland Co. | 1890-1897 | (68) |

"Wholesale Manufacturers of FURNITURE of EVERY DESCRIPTION. Bedroom Suits and Parlour Suits a Specialty. E. A. King, Manager."

| | | | |
|---|---|---|---|
| EWING, JOSEPH | Halifax, Halifax Co. | 1826 | (29) |

FARISH, GEORGE Yarmouth Township 1827 (12)

FARNHAM, REUBEN Cornwallis, Kings Co. —1864-1869— (47-49)
Canard Street, Cornwallis, about 6 miles from Kentville.

FARNHAM, W. N. Halifax, Halifax Co. 1826 (29)

FENTON, DENNIS Halifax, Halifax Co. 1826 (29)

FENTON, WILLIAM Halifax, Halifax Co. 1866-1870 (47, 49-50)
Chairmaker. Resided in Dartmouth, carried on his business at No. 7-9
John Street in Halifax.

FIELDING, JAMES Halifax, Halifax Co. 1838-1863 (14, 45)
16 Blowers St. (1863)

FISHER, JAMES Halifax, Halifax Co. 1826 (29)

FLETCHER, CHARLES River Philip, Cumberland Co. 1864-1865 (46)

FLETCHER, WILLIAM River Philip, Cumberland Co. 1864-1865 (46)

FOGARTY, J. Halifax, Halifax Co. 1887 (70)
A cabinetmaker in Gordon & Keith's factory.

FOSTER, ELIAS Guysboro, Guysboro Co. 1864-1865 (46)

FOSTER & ALLAN Amherst, Cumberland Co. 1890-1897 (68)
Burton Foster.
Andrew T. Allan.
"Church, Office, School, Bank and House Furniture."

FRAME, JAMES Halifax, Halifax Co. 1799-1810 (18)

FRANCIS, GEORGE Halifax, Halifax Co. 1814 (72)
March 19, 1814 took out a marriage bond to marry Elizabeth Osborne,
spinster.

FRASER, THOMAS J. Halifax, Halifax Co. 1864-1867 (46, 47)
A cabinetmaker for W. Fraser & Sons.

FRASER, THOMAS R. Halifax, Halifax Co. 1831 (33)
Furniture painter.

FRASER, WILLIAM & SONS Halifax, Halifax Co. 1858-1897 (45, 45A, 47,
Thomas J. Fraser. 49-68)
William Fraser.
William Fraser, Jr., was foreman cabinetmaker. (1890-97)
70-71 Barrington St. (1858-59)
57 Barrington St. (1863)
70 Barrington St. (1866-67). Cabinetmakers & Upholsterers.
70-72 Barrington St. (1868-72)
82-84 Barrington St. (1873-90)
78-80 Granville St. (1890-97. Furniture manufacturers.

FREDERICKS, JAMES E. Truro, Colchester Co. 1890-1897 (68)

FRIZZLE, A. M. Halifax, Halifax Co. 1884 (62)

FULLERTON, DAVID Pictou, Pictou Co. 1864-1880 (46-47, 69)
Furniture manufacturer on Coleraine St.

FULTZ, CONNOLLY Bridgewater, Lunenburg Co. 1864-1869 (46, 48)

GAMMON, GEORGE        Cole Harbour, Halifax Co.     —1838-1859      (14)
     Chairmaker.

GARDE, JAMES        Halifax, Halifax Co.      1864-1869     (46, 47, 49)

GARRETT, FRANK        New Glasgow, Pictou Co.     —1879-1897—     (68, 69)
     In 1879 he was upholsterer for Cumming Brothers' furniture factory; but in 1890-97 he is listed as "manufacturer and dealer in Furniture of every description" at 58 Provost St.

GASS, JOSEPH        Pictou Township, Pictou Co.     1838      (15)

GASS, ROBERT        Pictou Township, Pictou Co.     1838      (15)

GATES, MARTIN        Port George, Annapolis Co.     1864-1865      (46)

GATLE, EMANUEL        Halifax, Halifax Co.      1864-1865      (46)

GEDDES, ROBERT        Halifax, Halifax Co.      1780      (74)

GEORGE, ....        Halifax, Halifax Co.      1785      (4)

GIBBS, ATKIN        Halifax, Halifax Co.      1776      (3)

GILLIS, J.        Halifax, Halifax Co.      1887      (70)
     A cabinetmaker at Gordon & Keith's factory.

GODDARD,        Shelburne, Shelburne Co.     1786-1788      (7, 8)
  DANIEL, HENRY, JOB     Halifax, Halifax Co.
     They are on Water Street in Shelburne in 1786 and are listed as "Cabinet Makers." However, in the assessment roll of 1787 they are on Fanning Lane and listed as "carpenters."

GODDARD, DANIEL        Digby, Digby Co.      —1819—

GORDON, E. W.        New Glasgow, Pictou Co.     1879-1880      (69)
     Provost Street.

GORDON, JAMES        Halifax, Halifax Co.
     In 1854 he carried on the business of Cabinetmaker and Upholsterer at 123 Barrington Street, south of Saint Paul's Church.
     (SEE GORDON & KEITH)

GORDON, WILLIAM        Halifax, Halifax Co.     —1814-1838—     (14, 29, 72)

GORDON & KEITH        Halifax, Halifax Co.      1860-1960     (15, 19-68)
     James Gordon.
     Donald Keith.
     Alexander Keith.
     Cabinetmakers and furniture manufacturers. Factory at 17-23 Dundonald St.
        33-37 Barrington St. (1863)
        37 Barrington St. (1868-72)
        41-45 Barrington St. (1873-97)

GRANT, WM.        Halifax, Halifax Co.      1864-1865      (46)

GREENLAUGH, W. H.        Halifax, Halifax Co.      1884      (62)

GRIEVE, THOMAS        Liverpool, Queens Co.     1864-1869      (47, 49)

GUARD, JAMES        Halifax, Halifax Co.      1866-1867      (47)
     (see also GARDE, JAMES)

| | | | |
|---|---|---|---|
| HALIBURTON, W. H. O. | Annapolis Royal, Annapolis Co. | 1864-1869 | (46, 47, 49) |
| HAINEY, JOHN | Halifax, Halifax Co. | 1884 | (62) |
| HALL, DAVID | Lunenburg, Lunenburg Co. | 1864-1869 | (49) |
| HALL, PETER | Halifax, Halifax Co. | 1864-1865 | (46) |
| HAMILTON, HUGH | Halifax, Halifax Co. | 1826 | (29) |
| HAMILTON, STEWART & CO. | Halifax, Halifax Co. | 1817 | (25) |
| HANDWRIGHT, WILLIAM | Tidnish Cross Roads, Cumberland Co. | 1864-1865 | (46) |
| HARDWICK, ADELBERT | Yarmouth, Yarmouth Co. | 1864-1865 | (46) |
| HARLOW, ROBERT | Bridgetown, Annapolis Co. | 1890-1897 | (68) |
| HARRISON, HENRY | Halifax, Halifax Co. | 1826 | (29) |
| HARRISON, JOHN | Halifax, Halifax Co. | 1864-1867 | (46-47) |

HARRISON, THOMAS (1816-64)   Halifax, Halifax Co.   1840-1864

Came from England. He made the patterns for the lion's head on the Halifax County Court House. He was associated with his sons Thomas and John in owning a mill on the North West Arm.

HARRISON, W.   Halifax Co.   1848   (41)

He had a furniture factory on the road to St. Margaret's Bay.

HART, ARCHIBALD   Pictou, Pictou Co.   1847   (40)

HARVEY, JOHN   Halifax, Halifax Co.   —1887—   (70)

In 1887 he had been employed as a cabinetmaker at the factory of Gordon & Keith for twenty years.

HEFFERNAN, A.   Halifax, Halifax Co.   1887   (70)

A cabinetmaker at Gordon & Keith's factory.

HEFFERNAN, EDWARD   Halifax, Halifax Co.   —1831-1838—   (14, 33)

A cabinetmaker and chairmaker. The *Acadian Recorder* of February 12, 1831 said that he was on "Duke Street, adjoining Mr. M'Dougall's."

HEFFERNAN, W. E.   Halifax, Halifax Co.   —1864-1879   (46, 49-58)

"Manufacturer and Importer of Household Furniture, Feathers, Mattresses, British and American Looking Glasses."
        13 Prince St. (1868-72)
        12 Prince St. (1873-74)
        14-16 Prince St. (1875-77)
        24-26 Sackville St. (1877-79)
Mary Heffernan, widow of Edward, is listed in 1880-81.

HEGAN, W. J.   Bass River, Colchester Co.   1890-1897   (68)

Chairmaker.

HENESSEY, JOHN   Halifax, Halifax Co.   1864-1865   (46)

HEPBURN, GEORGE   Pictou, Pictou Co.   1879-1880   (69)

He will make to order "Wardrobes, Bureaus, Book Cases, Tables, Doors, Sashes."

HEWBAULT, WILLIAM   Halifax, Halifax Co.   1868-1869   (49)

| | | | |
|---|---|---|---|
| HEUSTUS, JAMES | Yarmouth, Yarmouth Co. | 1864-1869 | (46, 49) |
| HEUSTUS, JOSHUA | Yarmouth, Yarmouth Co. | 1864-1869 | (46, 49) |
| HEUSTUS, NATHAN | Yarmouth, Yarmouth Co. | 1864-1869 | (46, 49) |
| HEUSTUS, WILLIAM E. | Yarmouth, Yarmouth Co. | 1868-1869 | (49) |
| HEUSTUS & MOULTON (see also HUESTIS) | Yarmouth, Yarmouth Co. | 1868-1869 | (49) |
| HICKEY, JAMES | Halifax, Halifax Co. | 1864-1865 | (46) |
| HICKEY, P. | Halifax, Halifax Co. | 1887 | (70) |

A cabinetmaker at Gordon & Keith's factory.

| | | | |
|---|---|---|---|
| HICKEY & SON | Halifax, Halifax Co. | 1882-1887 | (60-64) |

Francis Hickey.
James Hickey.
James F. Hickey.
Lawrence Hickey.
Patrick Hickey.
William Hickey.

| | | | |
|---|---|---|---|
| HILL, JOHN | Amherst, Cumberland Co. | 1864-1897 | (46, 49, 68) |
| HILL, OWEN | Truro, Colchester Co. | 1890-1897 | (68) |
| HILL, THEODORE | Truro, Colchester Co. | 1890-1897 | (68) |
| HILLS, JAMES C. | Halifax, Halifax Co. | 1864-1869; 1871-1874 | (47, 49, 52-53) |

"Cabinetmaker, Upholsterer, and Undertaker. Manufactures furniture polish."
     82-84 Barrington St. (1871-72)
     106 Argyle St. (1873-74)

| | | | |
|---|---|---|---|
| HILLS & BRUSH | Halifax, Halifax Co. | 1868-1870 | (49, 50) |

"Cabinet Makers, Upholsterers, and Undertakers, No. 82 Barrington St., one door south of Chalmers' Church, Halifax, N.S. Manufacturers of all kinds of Drawing Room, Dining, and Bed Room Furniture . . . continue to manufacture their celebrated *Furniture Polish.*"
James C. Hills.
James P. Brush.

| | | | |
|---|---|---|---|
| HILTZ, ALBERT | Truro, Colchester Co. | 1890-1897 | (68) |
| HIRTLE, GEORGE | Lunenburg, Lunenburg Co. | 1864-1869 | (46, 49) |
| HOBSON, JOHN | Halifax, Halifax Co. | 1884 | (62) |
| HOGG & GEDDES | Halifax, Halifax Co. | 1783 | (4) |
| HOLDER, THOMAS | Halifax, Halifax Co. | 1864-1869 | (46, 49) |
| HOLDER, THOMAS C. 59 Brenton St. | Halifax, Halifax Co. | 1890-1897 | (68) |
| HOLDER & SON | Halifax, Halifax Co. | 1883-1890 | (61-67) |

Henry A. Holder.
James Holder.
Thomas C. Holder.
     129 Hollis St.

| | | | |
|---|---|---|---|
| HOLLAND, WILLIAM | Truro Road, Halifax Co. | 1838 | (14) |
| HOLZOMER, EDWARD | New Glasgow, Pictou Co. | 1879-1880 | (69) |

Furniture painter.

| | | | |
|---|---|---|---|
| HOMER, ANDREW | Barrington Township, Shelburne Co. | 1838 | (15) |
| HOOP, JULIUS H. | Stewiacke Cross Roads, Colchester Co. | 1864-1869— | (46, 47, 49) |
| HOOPER, FRANCIS | Guysboro, Guysboro Co. | 1864-1867 | (46, 47) |
| HORTON, WILLIAM | Halifax, Halifax Co. | 1887 | (70) |

Cabinetmaker at Gordon & Keith's factory.

| | | | |
|---|---|---|---|
| HOWARD, RICHARD | Halifax, Halifax Co. | 1833 | (73) |

On January 29, 1833 he took out a marriage bond to marry Margaret Gordon, spinster.

| | | | |
|---|---|---|---|
| HOWE, MARTIN | St. Mary's Bay, Digby Co. | 1864-1869 | (46, 47, 49) |
| HOYT, GEORGE | Bridgetown, Annapolis Co. | 1890-1897 | (68) |
| HUESTIS, EDWARD | Yarmouth, Yarmouth Co. | 1854, 1866-1867 | (47) |
| HUESTIS, GEORGE | Yarmouth, Yarmouth Co. | 1890-1897 | (68) |
| HUESTIS, JONATHAN | Yarmouth, Yarmouth Co. | 1866-1867 | (47) |
| HUESTIS, JOSHUA | Yarmouth, Yarmouth Co. | 1864-1897 | (46, 68) |

Upholsterer.

| | | | |
|---|---|---|---|
| HUESTIS, WILLIAM | Yarmouth, Yarmouth Co. | 1890-1897 | (68) |
| HUESTIS & MOULTON | Yarmouth, Yarmouth Co. | 1864-1867 | (46-47) |

(see also HEUSTUS)

| | | | |
|---|---|---|---|
| HURLEY, THOMAS | Halifax, Halifax Co. | 1864-1865 | (46) |
| HUXTABLE, ROBERT C. | Dartmouth, Halifax Co. | 1866-1869 | (47, 49) |

King St.

| | | | |
|---|---|---|---|
| HUXTABLE, R. C. | Dartmouth, Halifax Co. | 1864-1878 | (46, 55, 56) |

Ochterloney St.
In 1878-79 is listed as a carpenter.

| | | | |
|---|---|---|---|
| INNES, GEORGE | Halifax, Halifax Co. | 1864-1865 | (46) |

He lived in Dartmouth.

| | | | |
|---|---|---|---|
| JAMISON, ROBERT | Halifax, Halifax Co. | 1838 | (14) |
| JESSENHOUSE, JOHN | Halifax, Halifax Co. | 1864-1869 | (46-47, 49) |
| JEWETT, JOSEPH | Halifax, Halifax Co. | 1793 | (9) |

Chairmaker.

| | | | |
|---|---|---|---|
| JOHNS, WILLIAM | Halifax, Halifax Co. | 1864-1869 | (46, 49) |
| JOHNSON, ALEX. | Halifax, Halifax Co. | 1812-1814 | (22, 72) |

David Wight & Alex. Johnson were cabinetmakers and upholsterers on the "lower side of the Parade, near the Post Office."

| | | | |
|---|---|---|---|
| JOHNSON, EDWARD | Halifax, Halifax Co. | 1890-1897 | (68) |

| | | | |
|---|---|---|---|
| JOHNSON, G.<br>City and Gerrish St. | Halifax, Halifax Co. | 1858-1859 | (45A) |
| JOHNSON, JOHN<br>St. Andrew's St. | Pictou, Pictou Co. | 1879-1880 | (69) |
| JOHNSTON, JOHN | Pictou, Pictou Co. | 1864-1865 | (46) |
| JOST, EDWARD<br>90 Argyle St. (1858-59)<br>58 Argyle St. (1863-72)<br>68 Argyle St. (1873-86) | Halifax, Halifax Co. | 1858-1886 | (45A, 45-47<br>49-64) |
| KEEFE, CHRISTOPHER | Roslin, Cumberland Co. | 1890-1897 | (68) |
| KEEFE, HERBERT | Oxford, Cumberland Co. | 1890-1897 | (68) |
| KEITH, DONALD (1832-1918)<br>(see GORDON & KEITH) | | | |
| KENNEDY, ROBERT | Halifax, Halifax Co. | 1864-1865 | (46) |
| KENT, ALEXANDER | Lower Stewiacke,<br>Colchester Co. | 1810 | (19) |
| Cabinetmaker, house joiner, wheelwright, and shipbuilder. | | | |
| KNUDLE, JOHN | Halifax, Halifax Co. | 1838 | (14) |
| KOCH, GEORGE JOSEPH | Halifax, Halifax Co. | 1826-1867 | (29, 47) |
| LAIDLAW, C.<br>A cabinetmaker at Gordon & Keith's factory. | Halifax, Halifax Co. | 1887 | (70) |
| LAIDLAW, JOHN | Halifax, Halifax Co. | 1864-1869 | (46, 49) |
| LAIDLAW, R.<br>A cabinetmaker at Gordon & Keith's factory. | Halifax, Halifax Co. | 1887 | (70) |
| LAMBERT, WESLEY | Bridgewater, Lunenburg Co. | 1864-1869 | (46, 49) |
| LAMBERT, WILLIAM<br>48 Buckingham St.<br>(see NEWCOMB & LAMBERT) | Halifax, Halifax Co. | 1868-1870 | (49, 50) |
| LAMBERT BROS.<br>George M. Lambert.<br>William Lambert.<br>265 Barrington St. (1875-76)<br>215 Barrington St. (1877-85) | Halifax, Halifax Co. | 1875-1885 | (54-63) |
| LANE, JOHN<br>Painter and gilder. | Bridgewater, Lunenburg Co. | 1868-1869 | (49) |
| LANGILLE, JOHN | Halifax, Halifax Co. | 1864-1869 | (46, 49) |
| LAURILLIARD, ALBERT | Pictou, Pictou Co. | 1839 | (36) |
| LAVERMAN, W.<br>(see also LEVERMAN, W.) | Halifax, Halifax Co. | 1838 | (14) |
| LAVERS, JUDSON A. | Windsor, Hants Co. | 1890-1897 | (68) |
| LAWRINSON, PERCY | Oxford, Cumberland Co. | 1890-1897 | (68) |

LAWRINSON, RUSSELL     Oxford, Cumberland Co.     1890-1897     (68)

LAWSON, RICHARD     Halifax, Halifax Co.     1783—     (4)

LESSEL, JAMES     Halifax, Halifax Co.     1864-1865     (46)

LEVERMAN, EMIL     Halifax, Halifax Co.     1864-1865     (46)

LEVERMAN, FREDERICK W.     Halifax, Halifax Co.     1875-1876     (55)
Employed by Williams & Leverman.

LEVERMAN, HENRY A.     Halifax, Halifax Co.     1866-1867     (47)

LEVERMAN, PHILIP     Halifax, Halifax Co.     1876-1877     (56)
Employed by Williams & Leverman, later had his own piano manufactory.

LEVERMAN, WILLIAM     Halifax, Halifax Co.     1858-1890     (45, 45A, 47, 54, 67)
    Dresden Row and Morris St. (1858-59)
    15 Dresden Row. (1863)
    160 Water St. (1866-67)
    11-15 Carleton St. (1873-)
(see also WILLIAMS & LEVERMAN)

LINDSAY, JOSEPH     Halifax, Halifax Co.     1864-1869     (46, 47, 49)

LOCKE, WILLIAM     Halifax, Halifax Co.     1887     (70)
Had been employed as a cabinetmaker at Gordon & Keith's factory for 20 years.

LOGAN, D. C.     New Glasgow, Pictou Co.     1890-1897     (68)
"manufacturer and dealer in Furniture, Parlour, Bedroom, and Dining Room Setts, Lounges."
    Provost St.

LONG, JAMES     Halifax, Halifax Co.     1864-1878     (46, 49-57)
    187 Grafton St. (1868-69)
    189 Grafton St. (1869-72)
    219 Grafton St. (1873-78).
Listed as a carpenter in 1877-78.

LONGARD, GEORGE     St. Margaret's Bay, Halifax Co.     1838     (14)

LOVETT, AMOS     Halifax, Halifax Co.     1793     (9)

LOW, BENJAMIN     Granville Township, Annapolis Co.     1838     (15)

LOW, JACOB     Granville Township, Annapolis Co.     1838     (15)

LOWNDS, THOMAS, JR.     Halifax, Halifax Co.     —1859-1865     (46)

LUNENBURG FURNITURE CO.     Lunenburg, Lunenburg Co.     —1893—
Incorporated in 1893 with Margaret McNeill, J. S. Meisner, Joshua Hirtle, and Thomas G. Nicol, with capital of $5,000.

LYNAGH, M.     Halifax, Halifax Co.     1864-1869, 1873-1886     (46, 47, 49 53-63)
    42 Cornwallis St. Not listed in 1886-87.

LYNAGH, MICHAEL     Halifax, Halifax Co.     1890-1897     (68)
    42 Cornwallis St.

LYNAGH, RICHARD      Halifax, Halifax Co.     1864-1867    (46, 47)
    47 Maitland St.

MCARTHUR, JOHN & CO.    Hopewell, Pictou Co.   —1879-1897   (68, 69)
    Teare's *Pictou Directory* for 1879-80 states that he has a sash, blind,
and furniture manufactory, and that "Furniture made and repaired."
In 1890 he is "manufacturer of the Celebrated *Grand-Daddy Arm
Chair*. Furniture, Doors, Windows, Blinds, Stair Posts and Ballusters
constantly on hand."

MCCULLOCH, GEORGE    Pictou, Pictou Co.    1810-1812    (19)
    A brother of the Rev. Thomas McCulloch, founder of Pictou Academy.

MCDONALD, GEORGE    Avondale, Pictou Co.   1890-1897   (68)

MCDONALD, J.      Halifax, Halifax Co.    1887    (70)
    A cabinetmaker at Gordon & Keith's factory.

MCEWAN & CO.      Halifax, Halifax Co.   —1863-1897  (45-47, 49 68)
    Andrew McEwan listed in 1863.
    Daniel McEwan listed from 1864 to 1873.
    James McEwan listed from 1864 to 1897.
        20 Barrington St. (1863-72)
        24 Barrington St. (1873-97)
    "Cabinet Makers & Upholsterers . . . First Class Cabinet Furniture,
design and estimates furnished on application . . . Prize Medal
Awarded Exhibition of 1862." Listed as upholsterers only in 1889-90.

MCEWAN & REID      Halifax, Halifax Co.    1862
    Exhibited furniture at the International Exhibition at London, England,
in 1862.

MCGOWAN, JOHN     New Glasgow, Pictou Co.  1879-1880   (69)
    Bridge St.

MCKAY, DONALD      New Glasgow, Pictou Co.  1890-1897   (68)

MCKEIL, J. J.       Halifax, Halifax Co.   1876-1879   (55-58)
    71 Barrington St. (1876-77)
    41 Argyle St. (1877-79)

MCLAREN, GEORGE    Pictou, Pictou Co.   —1864-1897—  (46, 49, 68-69)
    Falkland St. (1879-80)
    Water St. (1890-97)
    Furniture and undertaker.

MCLAREN, WILLIAM    Pictou, Pictou Co.   1831-1897   (34, 37, 49,
    Water St.                                              68-69)

MCLEOD, DONALD     Tidnish, Cumberland Co.  1864-1865   (46)

MCMASTERS, WILLIAM   Halifax, Halifax Co.   1821

MCMULLEN, JAMES    Shelburne, Shelburne Co.  1827    (12)

MCNEAL, ALEXANDER   Lunenburg Township   —1794—    (9)

MACK, SAMUEL      Bridgetown, Annapolis Co. 1890-1897   (68)

MAHON, WILLIAM     Halifax, Halifax Co.   1864-1869   (46, 49)

MALCOM, JAMES      Halifax, Halifax Co.   —1826-1838—  (14, 29)

| | | | |
|---|---|---|---|
| MAN(sic), JAMES | Halifax, Halifax Co. | 1826 | (29) |
| MANN, JAMES | Halifax, Halifax Co. | 1826 | (29) |
| MANN, WILLIAM | Halifax, Halifax Co. | 1864-1865 | (46) |
| MARSH, GEORGE | Portaupique, Colchester Co. | 1864-1869 | (46, 47, 49) |
| MARSHALL, JOHN | Aylesford, Kings Co. | 1864-1869 | (46, 47, 49) |
| MASON, JAMES | St. Margaret's Bay and Halifax, Halifax Co. | 1868-1870 | (49, 50) |

Wilson's Wharf, 301 Upper Water St.

| | | | |
|---|---|---|---|
| MATHIAS, JOHN | Halifax, Halifax Co. | 1866-1867 | (47) |
| MAXWELL, JAMES WILLIAM | New Glasgow, Pictou Co. | 1879-1880 | (69) |

Glasgow St.

| | | | |
|---|---|---|---|
| MIDDLEMAS, JAMES | Halifax, Halifax Co. | 1864-1865 | (46) |
| MILKIE, (MEIKLE), CHARLES | Halifax, Halifax Co. | 1864-1869 | (46, 47, 49) |
| MISENER, GEORGE | Dartmouth, Halifax Co. | 1866-1867 | (47) |
| MISENER, JAMES | Dartmouth, Halifax Co. | 1864-1867 | (46, 47) |
| MISENER, JOHN | Dartmouth, Halifax Co. | —1863-1897 | (46, 68) |

Partner in Brockley, Misener & Brockley, pianoforte manufacturers in 1863, and in 1866-1867 had pianoforte and furniture warerooms on Barrington Street where "furniture of all descriptions always on hand or made to order at the shortest notice."

| | | | |
|---|---|---|---|
| MISENER, WILLIAM | Halifax, Halifax Co. | —1887— | (70) |

Had been employed as a cabinetmaker at Gordon & Keith's factory for twenty years.

| | | | |
|---|---|---|---|
| MOFFATT, JOHN | Halifax, Halifax Co. | 1866-1867 | (47) |
| MORASH, DOUGLAS | Chester, Lunenburg Co. | —1930— | |
| MORSE & TUPPER | Annapolis Royal, Annapolis Co. | 1866-1867 | (47) |
| MORTON, ARCHIBALD | Halifax, Halifax Co. | 1826-1838 | (14, 29) |
| MORTON, GEORGE | Halifax, Halifax Co. | —1887— | (70) |

Had been employed as a cabinetmaker at Gordon & Keith's factory for twenty years.

| | | | |
|---|---|---|---|
| MORTON, J. | Halifax, Halifax Co. | 1887 | (70) |

A cabinetmaker at Gordon & Keith's factory.

| | | | |
|---|---|---|---|
| MORTON, JAMES | Bridgewater, Lunenburg Co. | 1868-1869 | (49) |

Chairmaker.

| | | | |
|---|---|---|---|
| MOSER, EDWARD | Necum Teugh, Halifax Co. | 1864-1865 | (46) |
| MOSER, JOHN J. | Necum Teugh, Halifax Co. | 1864-1865 | (46) |
| MOULTON, E. D. | Yarmouth, Yarmouth Co. | —1881— | |
| MOULTON, S. E. | Yarmouth, Yarmouth Co. | 1864-1869 | (46, 49) |

Block and furniture maker.

| | | | |
|---|---|---|---|
| MUNRO, JAMES | Pictou Township, Pictou Co. | 1838 | (15) |
| MURPHY, MICHAEL | Halifax, Halifax Co. | 1866-1867 | (47) |

| | | | |
|---|---|---|---|
| MURPHY & O'BRIEN | Morristown, Kings Co. | 1864-1869 | (46, 47, 49) |
| NAUFTS, STEWART | Halifax, Halifax Co. | —1887— | (70) |

Had been employed as a cabinetmaker at Gordon & Keith's for twenty years.

| | | | |
|---|---|---|---|
| NAUGLE, EDWARD | Halifax, Halifax Co. | 1864-1869 | (46, 47, 49) |
| NEWCOMB, GEORGE C. | Halifax, Halifax Co. | 1864-1869; 1875-1897 | (46, 49, 54-68) |

"Every description of Furniture on hand or made to order . . ."
"Upholsterer, Manufacturer and Importer of Household Furniture."
    197 Barrington St. (1875-1886)
    263 Barrington St. (1889-1897)

| | | | |
|---|---|---|---|
| NEWCOMB & LAMBERT | Halifax, Halifax Co. | 1871-1874 | (52-53) |

    175 Barrington St.
"Cabinetmakers, Upholsterers, and Undertakers."
G. C. Newcomb
John Newcomb
L. C. Newcomb
G. M. Lambert
William Lambert

| | | | |
|---|---|---|---|
| NEW GLASGOW FURNITURE & WOODENWARE CO. | New Glasgow, Pictou Co. | 1884 | (62) |
| NICHOLS, HENRY A. | Bridgetown, Annapolis Co. | 1890-1897 | (68) |
| NOVA SCOTIA FURNISHING CO. | Halifax, Halifax Co. | 1890-1927 | |

Successors to A. Stephen & Son, 1890.

| | | | |
|---|---|---|---|
| NYE, A. K. G. | Halifax, Halifax Co. | 1868-1869, 1876 | (49, 55) |

    Furniture painter.

| | | | |
|---|---|---|---|
| NYE, WILLIAM | Halifax, Halifax Co. | 1868-1869 | (49) |

    Furniture painter.

| | | | |
|---|---|---|---|
| OATES, JOHN | Pictou, Pictou Co. | 1841 | (37) |
| O'CONNELL, DANIEL J. | Halifax, Halifax Co. | 1866-1867 | (47) |

    Furniture painter.

| | | | |
|---|---|---|---|
| O'DONNELL, CHARLES | Halifax, Halifax Co. | 1864-1869; 1876-1879 | (45, 49, 55-57) |
| OLDMIXON, EDMUND | Wyse's Corner, Halifax Co. | —1850— | |
| OXFORD FURNITURE CO. LTD. | Oxford, Cumberland Co. | 1890-1897 | (68) |

    J. H. Treen, manager.
    "Wholesale Manufacturers of Dining Room, Chamber & Parlour
    Furniture."

| | | | |
|---|---|---|---|
| PALLISTER, THOMAS | Halifax, Halifax Co. | —1812— | (21) |

    In February, 1812, he was doing business "in Hollis Street, nearly
    opposite Mr. Merrick's."
(see also TULLES, PALLISTER & M'DONALD)

| | | | |
|---|---|---|---|
| PARKER, JAMES & SON | Halifax, Halifax Co. | 1890-1897 | (68) |

    26-34 Jacob St.

| | | | |
|---|---|---|---|
| PATTERSON, HUGH | Steam Mill Village, Kings Co. | 1864-1865 | (46) |
| PAULAN, SAMUEL | Pictou, Pictou Co. | 1829 | |
| PAULLAN, JAMES | Pictou, Pictou Co. | 1838 | (15) |
| PENDER, ROBERT | Halifax, Halifax Co. | 1864-1865 | (46) |
| PENDER, ROBERT | Pictou, Pictou Co. | 1868-1869 | (49) |
| PENDER, ROBERT A. | Halifax, Halifax Co. | 1864-1865 | (46) |
| PERRY, HENRY | Yarmouth, Yarmouth Co. | 1890-1897 | (68) |

PRINCE, JOHN      Halifax, Halifax Co.      1838      (14)
    Chairmaker.

| | | | |
|---|---|---|---|
| PUDDINGTON, O. W. | Windsor, Hants Co. | 1870 | |
| PURDY, JOHN | Halifax, Halifax Co. | 1864-1865 | (46) |
| RAFUSE, JAMES | Lunenburg, Lunenburg Co. | 1890-1897 | (68) |
| RAFUSE, JAMES, JR. | Lunenburg, Lunenburg Co. | 1890-1897 | (68) |

RAYMOND, RICHARD      Yarmouth, Yarmouth Co.      1864-1869      (47, 49)
    From Milton.

| | | | |
|---|---|---|---|
| REED & EMSLIE | Bridgetown, Annapolis Co. | 1857 | |
| REED, JOHN B. | Bridgetown, Annapolis Co. | 1858-1890 | (46, 47, 49) |

RENNIE, WILLIAM      Halifax, Halifax Co.      1887      (70)
    A cabinetmaker at Gordon & Keith's factory.

RHODES, CURRY & CO.      Amherst, Cumberland Co.      1887-1909      (68)
    Nathaniel Curry, President.
    N. A. Rhodes, Vice-President.
    J. Mark Curry, Secretary-Treasurer.
    Founded in 1877 as contractors and woodworking factory at Amherst.
    Merged with the Canada Car Company and Dominion Car Company
    of Montreal in 1909, the name was changed to Canadian Car and
    Foundry Company, Ltd.

| | | | |
|---|---|---|---|
| RICHARDSON, WILLIAM | Halifax, Halifax Co. | 1864-1865 | (46) |

RIGBY, JAMES J.      Halifax, Halifax Co.      1876-1877      (55, 56)
    83 Gerrish St.

RIDGEWAY, A. & CO.      Halifax, Halifax Co.      1869-1874      (50-53)
    Augustus Ridgeway.
    31 Brunswick St.
    "Successors to late T. J. Ridgeway," manufacturer of all kinds of
    drawing room, dining room, bedroom, library and counting house
    furniture."

RIDGEWAY, RUPERT      Halifax, Halifax Co.      1864-1869;
    217 Brunswick St.                            1876-1881      (46, 49, 51-58)

RIDGEWAY, THOMAS J.      Halifax, Halifax Co.      —1858-1869      (45A, 47, 49)
    31 Brunswick St.
    "Cabinet Maker, Upholsterer, and Undertaker, Brunswick Street,
    corner of Hurd's Lane."

| RIDGEWAY, W. | Halifax, Halifax Co. | 1863 | (45) |
29 Brunswick St.

| RILEY, J. | Halifax, Halifax Co. | 1887 | (70) |
A cabinetmaker at Gordon & Keith's factory.

| RIPPERT, A. | Halifax, Halifax Co. | 1887 | (70) |
A cabinetmaker at Gordon & Keith's factory.

| ROACH, GEORGE | Windsor, Hants Co. | 1890-1897 | (68) |
Chairmaker.

| ROBB, WALTER | Halifax, Halifax Co. | 1876 | (55) |

| ROBERTSON, WILLIAM | Halifax, Halifax Co. | 1876 | (55) |

| ROBINSON, JOHN, JR. | Granville Ferry, Annapolis Co. | 1864-1869 | (46, 47, 49) |

| RODDER, C. | Halifax, Halifax Co. | 1887 | (70) |
A cabinetmaker at Gordon & Keith's factory.

| ROGERS, JOHN | Nictaux Falls, Annapolis Co. | 1864-1865 | (46) |

| ROSS, HUGH & SONS | New Glasgow, Pictou Co. | 1879-1897 | (68, 69) |
31 McDonald St.
"New Glasgow Furniture Factory" in 1879.
"Undertaker, Funeral Director and Desk Manufacturer" in 1897.
Hugh, John and William Ross.

| ROSS, WILLIAM | Brooklyn, Hants Co. | 1868-1869 | (49) |

| RUDOLPH, JOHN | Head of St. Margaret's Bay, Halifax Co. | 1864-1869 | (46, 49) |

| RUSSELL, JOHN | Windsor, Hants Co. | 1868-1869 | (49) |

| RUSSELL, JOHN G. | Windsor, Hants Co. | 1864-1869 | (46,49) |

| SANDERS, CHARLES W. | Yarmouth, Yarmouth Co. | 1866-1869 | (47, 49) |
Picture mountings, upholstering, furniture made and repaired. Shop nearly opposite Baptist Church, Main St., Yarmouth, N.S.

| SCOTT, JAMES | Halifax, Halifax Co. | 1821-1838 | (14, 29) |
Cabinetmaker and upholsterer.
In 1821 applied for licence as auctioneer. He was born and brought up in Scotland, "and has been many years settled in this Town . . . giving employment to a great number of hands."

| SCOTT, PETER J. | Halifax, Halifax Co. | 1864-1869 | (46-47, 49) |

| SELLON, H. | Halifax, Halifax Co. | 1887 | (70) |
A cabinetmaker at Gordon & Keith's factory.

| SHARP, JAMES W. | Windsor, Hants Co. | 1890-1897 | (68) |

| SHEPPARD, GEORGE | Halifax, Halifax Co. | 1838-1869 | (14, 46-47, 49) |

| SHERBROOKE, THOMAS | Halifax, Halifax Co. | 1866-1867 | (47) |

| SIBLEY, JOSEPH (b. 1790) | Wittenburg, Colchester Co. | —1830— | |
Chairmaker.

| SIBLEY, MICHAEL | Lower Stewiacke, Colchester Co. | —1856-1869— | (46, 47, 49) |
Chairmaker. In 1868 he was making 50 spinning jennies.

SIBLEY BROS.                    Wittenburg, Colchester Co.      1878-1900—    (68)
Chair manufacturers, also manufactured venetian blinds.
Aaron Sibley.
Ezekiel T. Sibley, manager.
Richard Sibley.
William Sibley.

SINCLAIR, CHARLES H.           Halifax, Halifax Co.            1864-1874     (46, 49-53)
"Manufacturer of all kinds of Household, Library, and Counting
House Furniture . . . Funerals Attended To."
    34 Barrington St. (1868-1872)
    42 Barrington St. (1873-1874)

SMART, ALEXANDER               New Glasgow, Pictou Co.        —1926-1931—    (76)

SMART, H.                      Halifax, Halifax Co.           1887          (70)
A cabinetmaker at Gordon & Keith's factory.

SMITH,    "from London."  Halifax, Halifax Co.               1821
*Weekly Chronicle* of December 21, 1821 says he is an "undertaker,
upholsterer, cabinet and chairmaker, Upper Water St., Halifax."

SMITH, DAVID                   Halifax, Halifax Co.           1810          (19)

SMITH, DAVID D.                Halifax, Halifax Co.           1864-1869     (46, 47, 49)
    162 Albemarle St.

SMITH, HENRY                   Wallace, Cumberland Co.        1864-1869     (46, 47, 49)

SMITH, JAMES                   Halifax, Halifax Co.           1826          (29)

SMITH, SIMEON F.               Cape Sable Island,             1864-1865     (46)
                               Shelburne Co.
In 1868-1869 he is listed as a joiner.

SNYDER, WILLIAM                Conquerall Banks,              1868-1869     (48)
                               Lunenburg Co.

SPIERS, JOHN                   Shelburne, Shelburne Co.       1787-1789     (8)
    Hamond St.

STAIG, RICHARD                 Halifax, Halifax Co.           1765
April 24, 1765, he took out bond to marry Abigail Greenleaf.

STAYNER, HENRY                 Halifax, Halifax Co.           1826          (29)

STEPHEN, ALEXANDER             Halifax, Halifax Co.           1862-1890—    (47, 49-68)
Alexander Stephen, Sr., born in Rothes, Scotland, d. 1884.
Alexander Stephen, Jr., born March 9, 1845 in Halifax.

Stephen, Alexander, (1866-1870), furniture & woodenware manufacturer.
Stephen, Alexander & Son, 85-87 Barrington Street, manufacturer of
furniture and woodenware of every description from 1871 to 1890.
"Manufacturer and Wholesale Dealer in Pails, Tubs, Washboards,
Clothes Pins, Corn Brooms, Bedsteads, Cain (sic) & Wood Seat Chairs,
& Pine Furniture." Factory at Ellershouse, Hants County.

NOVA SCOTIA FURNISHING CO., incorporated 1890, were successors to
Alexander Stephen & Son, (1890-1895), at 101-103 Barrington Street,
then removed to 72-76 Barrington Street. Alexander Stephen, Jr. was
president of this company.

| | | | |
|---|---|---|---|
| STEWART, JOHN | Halifax, Halifax Co. | 1864-1869 | (46, 49) |
| STIRLING, JOHN | Halifax, Halifax Co. | 1826 | (29) |
| STOREY, JAMES | Halifax, Halifax Co. | 1826 | (29) |
| SULLIVAN, EDMUND | Truro, Colchester Co. | 1864-1869 | (46, 47, 49) |
| SUMMERS, THOMAS | Halifax, Halifax Co. | 1864-1865 | (46) |
| SWEENEY, JACOB | Yarmouth, Yarmouth Co. | 1890-1897— | (68) |

Furniture manufacturer at 495-499 Main Street.

| | | | |
|---|---|---|---|
| TAYS, JAMES | Upper Musquodoboit, Halifax Co. | 1838 | (14) |
| THOMPSON, JAMES | Halifax, Halifax Co. | —1838— | (14) |
| THOMPSON, JAMES | Windsor, Hants Co. | 1864-1869 | (46, 49) |
| THOMSON, JAMES | Halifax, Halifax Co. | —1826-1867 | (29, 30, 45A, 47) |

In September 1826 the partnership of Alexander & Thomson was dissolved, and in February 1827 he was in business at No. 51 Barrington St., and later founded the firm of Thomson & Esson "who were the leading cabinetmakers of the City for many years," according to *Annals of North British Society, 1768-1903*. His partner, George Esson, died January 2nd, 1886. About 1860 they sold the firm to James Gordon and Donald Keith.

| | | | |
|---|---|---|---|
| TOWNSAND, JOHN | Windsor Township, Hants Co. | 1838 | (15) |
| TRAISE(?), A. | Halifax, Halifax Co. | 1887 | (70) |

A cabinetmaker at Gordon & Keith's factory.

| | | | |
|---|---|---|---|
| TULLES, JOHN | Halifax, Halifax Co. | —1811-1826— | (22, 29) |

In October, 1812 he removed to the house "lately occupied by Mrs. Gracie, and nearly opposite the Ordnance Gate," according to the *Halifax Journal* of January 25, 1813. His daughter, Jane, was baptized in St. Matthew's Presbyterian Church in Halifax on September 30, 1810 and his son, John, on August 23, 1812.

| | | | |
|---|---|---|---|
| TULLES, PALLISTER & M'DONALD | Halifax, Halifax Co. | 1810-1811 | (19) |

Cabinetmakers and upholsterers on Barrington Street "one door south of Sackville-street" (N.S. *Royal Gazette*, June 18, 1810).
John Tulles.
Thomas Pallister.
M'Donald.

| | | | |
|---|---|---|---|
| TURNER, DANIEL | Halifax, Halifax Co. | 1814-1816 | (23, 24) |
| TURNER, DAVID | Halifax, Halifax Co. | 1815 | (72) |

On August 28, 1815 he took out a marriage bond to marry Deborah Fitzgerald, spinster.

| | | | |
|---|---|---|---|
| TURPLE, STEPHEN | Halifax, Halifax Co. | 1866-1867 | (47) |
| WADDLE, JAMES (1764-1851) | Truro, Colchester Co. and South Maitland, Hants Co. | 1813-1851 | |
| WALLER, H. | Halifax, Halifax Co. | 1887 | (70) |

A cabinetmaker at Gordon & Keith's factory.

| | | | |
|---|---|---|---|
| WALSH, EDWARD | Halifax, Halifax Co. | 1868-1869 | (49) |
| WALSH, JAMES<br>225 Albemarle St. | Halifax, Halifax Co. | 1864-1867 | (46, 47) |

WARD, EDWARD          Halifax, Halifax Co.      —1887—      (70)
He had been employed as a cabinetmaker at Gordon & Keith's factory for twenty years.

WARD, K.                Halifax, Halifax Co.      1887        (70)
A cabinetmaker at Gordon & Keith's factory in 1887.

WARR, WILLIAM          Windsor, Hants Co.        1890-1897   (68)

WELBY, THYN & CO.      Pictou, Pictou Co.        1829        (32)

WESTHAVER, G. A.       Mahone Bay, Lunenburg Co. 1866-1869   (47, 49)
Carver and gilder, manufacturer of ships' blocks, house furniture, etc. "Furniture of every description manufactured and repaired. Always on hand—Sofas, Couches, Tables, Bureaus, What Nots, Wash Stands, Bedsteads & . . ."

WEYMOUTH INDUSTRIES    Weymouth, Digby Co.       1953—
Established in 1939 to manufacture Fairmile subchasers for Royal Canadian Navy during World War II. Re-opened in 1953 by a new company of Nova Scotian businessmen to build boats and furniture. Plant destroyed by fire, February 6, 1958, but re-opened in October of that year.

WHITE, JOHN           Amherst, Cumberland Co.   1864-1865   (46)

WIGHT (sic) & JOHNSON  Halifax, Halifax Co.      1812-1813   (22)
Cabinetmakers and upholsterers "lower side of the Parade, near the Post Office."
David Wight.
Alexander Johnson.

WILE, AUGUSTUS         Bridgewater, Lunenburg Co. 1868-1869  (49)
Chairmaker.

WILE, ZERAH           Bridgewater, Lunenburg Co. 1866-1869  (47, 49)
"He is prepared to fill orders for wood seated chairs of every description." Ad shows a most elaborately carved upholstered arm chair, lion mask and claws, shell on seat rail.

WILLIAMS, LEONARD     New Glasgow, Pictou Co.   —1926-1931— (76)

WILLIAMS & LEVERMAN   Halifax, Halifax Co.      1864-1879   (46-47, 49 57)
William Williams.
Henry A. Leverman.
Wood Turning and Scroll Sawing, manufacturers of school and house furniture, later manufactured pianofortes.
160 Upper Water St. (1866-1872)
 25 Carleton St. (1873-1874)
 11-15 Carleton St. (1875-1879)

WILLIAMS & WARD       Halifax, Halifax Co.      1875-1876   (55)
Charles Williams.
Edward Ward.

WILSON, CALVIN                Carlton, Yarmouth Co.           1866-1869       (47, 49)

WILSON, CHARLES              Pictou, Pictou Co.               1842-1897       (38, 49, 68, 69)
Apprenticed to Thomson & Esson of Halifax, in the early years of his
career he was associated with W. MacLaren of Pictou. In 1868-1869 he
was living on Water Street; in 1879-1880 he was listed on Church Street
and in 1890 he was cabinetmaker and undertaker.

WILSON, JAMES F.             Dartmouth, Halifax Co.           1864-1869       (46, 49)

WILSON, J. & CO.             Halifax, Halifax Co.             1868-1874       (49-53)
(late WILSON & NEWCOMB)
57 Barrington St.
John Wilson.
Newcomb.
Cabinetmakers and Upholsterers, "All sizes of Ship Wheels," "Walnut
and Mahogany Sofas, Chairs, Couches."

WILSON & NEWCOMB             Halifax, Halifax Co.             1863-1867       (45, 47)
103-105 Argyle St.
John Wilson.
Newcomb
Walnut and mahogany sofas, chairs, couches, dining tables, sideboards,
bedsteads, wardrobes, bureaus, cottage bedsteads, cane and wood
seat chairs. "Every description of Furniture made to order at the
shortest notice."

WINDSOR FURNITURE CO.        Windsor, Hants Co.               1871-1897—      (68, 71)
A. P. Shand.
F. A. Shaw.
Clifford Shand.
Manufacturers of Cane and Wood Seat Chairs, Bedsteads, Tables, Bed
room Suites, etc. Incorporated in 1891 with a capital of $49,000 and
Andrew P. Shand, Edward W. Dimock, John Keith, Thomas Aylward,
William H. Blanchard, and Frederick A. Shand as directors.

WINDSOR RATTAN CO.           Windsor, Hants Co.               1890-1897       (68)
Jas. E. Smith, Manager.
A. J. Lawrence, Secretary and Treasurer.
Manufacturers of reed and rattan furniture, children's carriages.

WOODS, JOHN                  Halifax, Halifax Co.             1864-1869       (46, 47, 49)

WRIGHT, CHARLES              Liverpool Township, Queens Co.   1838            (15)
Upholsterer.

WRIGHT & ADAMS               Halifax, Halifax Co.             1814            (23)
Charles Wright.
T. G. S. Adams.

WYMAN, CALVIN                Carleton, Yarmouth Co.           1866-1869       (47, 49)

WYMAN, CALVIN & SON          Yarmouth, Yarmouth Co.           1864-1869       (46, 49)
Chair and cabinetmakers, also "manufacturers of Wyman's celebrated
Balanced Washing Machines. These Machines can be easily worked by
children 7 or 8 years of age."

WYMAN, CHARLES               Carleton, Yarmouth Co.           1866-1867       (47)

| | | | |
|---|---|---|---|
| WYMAN, JOHN C. | Yarmouth, Yarmouth Co. | 1864-1865 | (46) |
| WYMAN, JOSEPH | Yarmouth, Yarmouth Co. | 1864-1865 | (46) |
| WYMAN, W. H. | Yarmouth, Yarmouth Co. | 1864-1869 | (46, 49) |

Chair and cabinetmaker.

**WYMAN BROS.**  Carleton and Yarmouth,  1871-1883
Amos Hilton  Yarmouth Co.
Joseph R. Wyman.
William H. Wyman.
Their furniture factory at Carleton destroyed by fire February 28, 1878 with loss of $10,000.

WYMAN & FREEMAN        Liverpool, Queens Co.        1864-1865        (46)

# APPENDIX B

*A list of chairmakers in Nova Scotia.*

**ACADIA CHAIR FACTORY**        Portaupique, Colchester Co.        —1870
Purchased by the Dominion Chair Company of Bass River, Col. Co.

**ALLEN, CHARLES P.**        Halifax, Fall River and        —1832-1862—        (14, 17, 33)
                             Waverley, Halifax Co.
He advertised a "good warranted Windsor Chair" for three shillings in 1849.  He became a British citizen in 1848.

**ALLEN & FENTON**        Halifax, Halifax Co.        1858-1859        (45A)
                          opposite Long Wharf.

**BLAIKIE, RICHARD**        Green Hill, Pictou Co.        —1887—
Grand-daddy easy chairs.

BOND, JOHN        Halifax, Halifax Co.        1792-1793        (9, 11)
BRITTAIN, JOHN        Halifax, Halifax Co.        1792        (9)

**BRITTAN, SEWELL W.**        Truro Road & Waverley,        1835-1847—
                             Halifax Co.
He was a native of Leominster, Massachusetts, and took the Oath of Allegiance to Queen Victoria on July 13, 1847.

**COLE, GEORGE**        Centre Rawdon, Hants Co.        —1832-1859        (15)
(c. 1808-1859.  Son of James Cole, q.v.)

**COLE, J.**        Halifax, Halifax Co.        1816        (24)
"Windsor and Grecian Chair-Maker."

**COLE, JAMES**        Centre Rawdon, Hants Co.        —1817-1827—
Came to Nova Scotia from the United States, of Scottish extraction.

**CUMMING, ANDREW**        Halifax, Halifax Co.        1792-1794        (9, 11)
Had a shop in Granville Street, according to the *Weekly Chronicle* of September 13, 1794.

CUTTER & POWER                Halifax, Halifax Co.            1814        (23)
   Chairs stamped.

DEGANT, ...... ....            Halifax, Halifax Co.            1780
   Chairs stamped.

DOMINION CHAIR COMPANY        Bass River, Colchester Co.      1860 to present

FENTON, WILLIAM               Halifax, Halifax, Co.           1866-1870   (47, 49-50)
   Chair maker. Resided in Dartmouth, carried on his business at No. 7-9
John Street in Halifax.

GAMMON, GEORGE                Cole Harbour, Halifax Co.       —1838-1859—  (14)
   Chairs stamped.

HEFFERNAN, EDWARD             Halifax Co.                     —1831-1838—  (14, 33)
   The *Acadian Recorder* of February 12, 1831 said that he was on "Duke
Street adjoining Mr. M'Dougall's," and "as he imports no Chairs from
the United States, he can recommend his as very superior to any made
by machinery."

HEGAN, W. J.                  Bass River, Colchester Co.      1890-1897   (68)

HUMESTON, JOY                 Halifax, Halifax Co.            1805-1815   (23)
   Chairs stamped.   Windsor style Bamboo chairs, settees.

JEWETT, JOSEPH                Halifax, Halifax Co.            1793        (9)

LAVERS, JUDSON A.             Windsor, Hants Co.              1890-1897   (68)

MCARTHUR, JOHN                Hopewell, Pictou Co.            —1879-1897—  (68, 69)
   "Manufacturer of the Celebrated Grand-daddy Arm Chair."

MCFEAT & STEWART              Halifax, Halifax Co.            1817        (25)
   Rush and cane bottom chairs.

MCFEAT, W.                    Halifax, Halifax Co.            1818

MCLEOD, GEORGE                Cross Roads, Pictou Co. and     —1860—
                            Halifax, Halifax Co.
   A carver, he made the chairs in the Province House at Halifax for the
Legislative Councillors, but he is best known as a carver of figure heads
for vessels.

MACMILLAN, A. H.              Halifax, Halifax Co.            —1939—
   He carved the Royal Chair for Province House in 1939.

MINARD, ELIJAH               Liverpool Township, Queens Co.   1767-1805

MORTON, JAMES                 Bridgewater, Lunenburg Co.      1868-1869   (49)

PRINCE, JOHN                  Halifax, Halifax Co.            1838        (14)

SIBLEY, JOSEPH                Wittenburg, Colchester Co.      —1830—
   (born 1790.)   Chairs stamped.

SIBLEY, MICHAEL               Lower Stewiacke, Colchester Co.—1856-1869—   (47, 49)
   The fourth son of Joseph Sibley. In 1868 he was making spinning
jennies.

SIBLEY BROS.          Lower Stewiacke, Colchester Co.—1878-1900—    (68)
E. T. Sibley was manager. The factory was at Wittenburg, and the furniture was shipped from the railway station at Lower Stewiacke. In business were Aaron, Benjamin, Edward George, Richard, Stephen, and William Sibley.

SMITH, ......... "from London"    Halifax, Halifax Co.        1821

STEPHEN, ALEXANDER       Halifax, Halifax Co.       1862-1870    (49, 50)
In these years he was primarily a chair manufacturer, but from 1871 to 1890 he manufactured furniture and woodenware of every description. Had factories at Fall River, Halifax County, and Ellershouse in Hants County.

WADE, JOHN           Granville, Annapolis Co.      1760-1813
"The first turning-lathe in the country was introduced by him."

WHITMAN & BEST        Halifax, Halifax Co.        1827
Windsor chairs.

WILE, AUGUSTUS        Bridgewater, Lunenburg Co.   1868-1869    (49)

WILE, ZERAH           Bridgewater, Lunenburg Co.   1866-1869    (47, 49)
"He is prepared to fill orders for wood seated chairs of every description."

WYMAN, CALVIN         Carleton, Yarmouth Co.     1868-1869    (49)

WYMAN, CALVIN & SON    Yarmouth, Yarmouth Co.    1868-1869    (49)

WYMAN, W. H.          Yarmouth, Yarmouth Co.    1868-1869    (49)

WYMAN & TILLEY       Yarmouth, Yarmouth Co.    1853—
Melzar J. Wyman.
Chair and cabinetmaking.

# APPENDIX C

*A list of the cabinetmakers, joiners, and turners who came to Halifax with Governor Cornwallis in June, 1749.*

*Charlton,* frigate.    Richard Townsend, joiner; Edward Boswell, joiner; Richd. Jones, turner.

*Winchelsea,* ship.    Edward Draper, cabinetmaker, single man.

*Wilmington,* ship.    Joseph Edwards, joyner; John Petty & wife, joyner; Moses Walwood, carpenter and joiner; Robt Kershaw & wife, carpenter and joiner; Thom. Groom & wife, joyner; and Thomas Noddell, joyner.

*Beaufort,* ship.    Philip Hemet, joyner; Thos. Dent & wife, turner.

*Canning,* ship.    Wm. Wilson & wife, turner.

*Everley,* ship.    John Woodin & wife, joiner; Thos. Gunan, joyner; Saml. Townsend & wife, joyner.

*Baltimore,* ship.    Wm. Wanson & wife, joyner; John Moseley, joyner.
William Craft, upholsterer, came on the *Winchelsea* in 1749. He was still in Halifax in 1752.

# APPENDIX D

*A list of joiners on the passenger lists of Foreign Protestants who came to Halifax from 1750 to 1753. Many later settled in Lunenburg.*

Anderson, George Frederick, 30, Dantzig, joiner, on *Speedwell*, 1752.

Bell, John Nicholaas, 48, Malheim, joiner, on *Sally*, 1752.

Berger, Jacob, 35, from Palatinate, joiner, on *Murdoch*, 1751.

Boullion, Adam, 31, Montbeliard, joiner, on *Speedwell*, 1752.

Bouteillier, Jean, 29, Montbeliard, joiner, on *Betty*, 1752.

Bouellier, Jean George, 50, Montbeliard, joiner, on *Sally*, 1752.

Carlin, Jean, 38, Montbeliard, joiner, on *Speedwell*, 1752.

Carling, Jean, 38, Montbeliard, joiner, on *Speedwell*, 1752.

Cleesattel, Christoph, 35, Wurtemberg, joiner, on *Gale*, 1751.

Coulon, Pierre, 46, Montbeliard, joiner, on *Betty*, 1752.

Coulon, Pierre, fils, 19, Montbeliard, joiner, on *Betty*, 1752.

Coulon, David, 17, Montbeliard, joiner, on *Betty*, 1752.

Gertzens, Gelle, 45, Vriesland, joiner, on *Speedwell*, 1751.

Gortlier, Laurence, 40, from Isbenbourg, joiner, on *Murdoch*, 1751

Gretaux, Jean George, 35, Montbeliard, joiner, *Sally*, 1752.

Haas, Andries, 19, from Wurtemberg, joiner, came on *Murdoch*, 1751.

Haase, Jacob, 47, Durlach, joiner, on *Pearl*, 1751.

Kensel, Jacob, 23, from Aschs, joiner, on *Murdoch*, 1751.

Knihnle, Hans George, 40, Wurtemberg, joiner, on *Sally* 1752.

Kohl, Fredrich Ludwig, joiner, on *Gale*, 1751.

Kohl, Johann Philip, joiner, on *Gale*, 1751.

Kreuger, Hans, 24, Hollstein, joiner, on *Speedwell*, 1752.

Langile, David, 25, Montbeliard, joiner, on *Betty*, 1752.

Langile, Leopold, 24, Montbeliard, joiner, on *Betty*, 1752.

Leau, George, 30, Montbeliard, joiner, on *Speedwell*, 1752.

Myer, Hans George, 39, Durlach, joiner, on *Pearl*, 1751.

Muller, Paul, 20, Dantzig, joiner, on *Sally*, 1752.

Orth, Valentine, 20, Palatinate, joiner, on *Gale*, 1752.

Petterquin, Jean, 28, Montbeliard, joiner, on *Betty*, 1752.

Schmidt, Rudolph, 40, Palatinate, joiner, on *Gale*, 1752.

Schuhman, Johann Jacob, 24, from Itstein, joiner, on *Gale*, 1751.

Shunter, Martin, 46, Franconia, joiner, on *Sally*, 1752.

Spiegel, Johan Casper, 26, Dantzick, joiner, on *Sally*, 1752.

Volelty, Johannes, 34, Heylsbach, joiner, on *Pearl*, 1751.

Volker, Andris, 37, from Stolberg, joiner, on *Murdoch*, 1751.

# APPENDIX E

*A list of some pianoforte makers in Nova Scotia.*

| Name | Place | Date | Ref. No. |
|------|-------|------|----------|
| ANDERSON, GEORGE | Halifax, Halifax Co. | 1866-1867 | (47) |
| BROCKLEY, MISENER & BROCKLEY | Halifax, Halifax Co. | 1857-1863 | (45) |

"Pianos, Melodeons, Harmoniums.'
Alfred W. Brockley.
Thomas Brockley.
John Misener.

| | | | |
|------|-------|------|----------|
| BROCKLEY & BROCKLEY | Halifax, Halifax Co. | 1864-1867 | (45, 47) |
| BROCKLEY & CO. | Halifax, Halifax Co. | 1868-1897 | (49-68) |

Alfred W. Brockley.
Thomas Brockley.

| | | | |
|------|-------|------|----------|
| CHUTE, HALL & CO. | Yarmouth, Yarmouth Co. | 1890-1897 | (68) |

Hiram E. Chute.
Thomas Hall.

| | | | |
|------|-------|------|----------|
| FRASER, W. & SONS | Halifax, Halifax Co. | 1856-1890 | (45, 47, 49-67) |

Prices for 8 models in 1866 ranged from £45 to £120.
"are constantly manufacturing and keep on hand first class double action Pianofortes" in advertisement of 1868-1869.
James A. Fraser.
William Fraser.
William Fraser, Jr.

| | | | |
|------|-------|------|----------|
| GATES BROS. | Melvern Square, Annapolis Co. | 1872-1882; | |
| Organ manufacturers. | Truro, Colchester Co. | 1882-1897— | |

| | | | |
|------|-------|------|----------|
| GATES BROS. | Halifax, Halifax Co. | 1880-1885 | (60-63) |

Organ manufacturers.
Charles E. Gates.
George Gates.
Wellesley J. Gates.

| | | | |
|------|-------|------|----------|
| GATES, W. & A. | Halifax, Halifax Co. | 1885-1897; | (67-68) |
| | Truro, Colchester Co. | 1882-1897— | |

Austin L. Gates.
Winslow J. Gates.
"Importers and Dealers in Pianos, Parlor and Church Organs."

| | | | |
|------|-------|------|----------|
| HARDY, LUSBY & CO. | Amherst, Cumberland Co. | | |
| HARRIS, JOHN | Dartmouth, Halifax Co. | 1866-1867 | (47) |
| HEPBURN, JAMES | Pictou, Pictou Co. | —1854-1860— | |

Organ builder.

| | | | |
|------|-------|------|----------|
| HOWELL, JACOB W. | Halifax, Halifax Co. | 1866-1867 | (47) |
| IRWIN, THOMAS | Halifax, Halifax Co. | 1866-1867 | (47) |

| JOHNSON, HENRY | Halifax, Halifax Co. | 1864-1865 | (46) |
|---|---|---|---|
| JOHNSON, JAMES | Halifax, Halifax Co. | 1864-1865 | (46) |
| JOHNSTON, WILLIAM | Halifax, Halifax Co. | 1866-1867 | (47) |
| LEVERMAN, SHAND & CO. | Halifax, Halifax Co. | 1882-1883 | (61) |
| LEVERMAN, P. WILLIAM | Halifax, Halifax Co. | 1883-1885 | (62-63) |
| LEVERMAN, P. W. | Halifax, Halifax Co. | 1885-1886 | (64) |
| LEVERMAN, P. W. & CO. | Halifax, Halifax Co. | 1889-1897 | (67) |

"Having purchased all the duplicate patterns of Pianos of Philips, and Fraser & Son, we can repair Pianos cheaper than any other house in the Province."
L. H. Leverman
P. W. Leverman.
William E. Leverman.

| LEVERMAN, WILLIAM | Halifax, Halifax Co. | 1875-1876 | (54) |
|---|---|---|---|

(see also WILLIAMS & LEVERMAN)

| MANTHORNE, WILLIAM | Bridgetown, Annapolis Co. | 1890-1897 | (68) |
|---|---|---|---|

Organ builder.

| MISENER, JOHN A. | Halifax, Halifax Co. | 1863-1867 | (45, 47) |
|---|---|---|---|

Pianoforte and furniture warerooms. "Furniture of all descriptions always on hand or made to order at the shortest notice."

| MISENER, JOHN A. | Dartmouth, Halifax Co. | 1890-1897 | (68) |
|---|---|---|---|
| MOIR, GEORGE | Halifax, Halifax Co. and Wilmot, Annapolis Co. | 1852-1865 | (46) |
| MURPHY, MICHAEL T. | Halifax, Halifax Co. | 1866-1867 | (47) |
| PHILIPS, H. & J. | Halifax, Halifax Co. | 1845-1859 | |

From Germany. Henry Philips; John B. Philips. On August 1, 1859 sold out to William Fraser and Sons.

| REED, JOHN BATH | Bridgetown, Annapolis Co. | 1881-1882— | |
|---|---|---|---|

Organ factory.

| SLADE, B. | Halifax, Halifax Co. | 1832 | |
|---|---|---|---|

From England. "Organ Builder and Piano Forte Maker."

| SLADE, RICHARD | Truro, Colchester Co. | 1866-1867 | (47) |
|---|---|---|---|

Organ builder.

| SPIKE, JAMES A. | Halifax, Halifax Co. | 1864-1867 | (46, 47) |
|---|---|---|---|
| WILLIAMS & LEVERMAN | Halifax, Halifax Co. | 1873-1890 | (53-67) |

Frederick W. Leverman.
Henry A. Leverman.
Henry Leverman, Jr.
William Leverman.
William Williams.

# APPENDIX F

*A list of some watch- and clockmakers of Nova Scotia to 1880.*

| Name | Place | Date | Ref. No. |
|---|---|---|---|
| ADAMS, THOMAS | Shelburne, Shelburne Co. | 1786-1787 | (8) |
| AGNEW, M. F. | Liverpool, Queens Co. | 1866-1867 | (47) |
| Dentist and watchmaker. | | | |
| ANDERSON, JOHN | New Glasgow, Pictou Co. | 1879-1880 | (69) |
| ANDERSON, ROBERT | Windsor, Hants Co. | 1816 | (24) |
| AUSTIN, MATTHEW L. | Halifax, Halifax Co. | 1866-1867 | (47) |
| BARRETT, MOSES | Yarmouth, Yarmouth Co. & Amherst, Cumberland Co. | 1830-1870 | |
| BECKER, IGNAZ | Halifax, Halifax Co. | 1877-1878 | (56) |
| BENNETT, JOHN B. | Halifax, Halifax Co. | 1873-1874 | (53) |
| BENNETT BROS. | Halifax, Halifax Co. | 1875-1876 | (54) |
| BESSONETT, J. S. | Halifax, Halifax Co. | —1827— | (12) |
| BIRD, THOS. H. | Halifax, Halifax Co. | 1873-1874 | (53) |
| BOLTON, THOMAS | Halifax, Halifax Co. | 1809-1838— | (14) |
| BROWN, HENRY | Halifax, Halifax Co. | 1838-1863 | (14) |
| BROWN, M. S. (1818-1886) & CO. | Halifax, Halifax Co. | 1840-1919 | (45, 47, 50, 54-58) |
| Firm was purchased by Henry Birks and Sons in 1919 | | | |
| BROWN, R. BALFOUR | Yarmouth, Yarmouth Co. | 1866-1867 | (47) |
| BROWNE, ALFRED | Halifax, Halifax Co. | 1866-1870 | (47, 50, 52) |
| BROWNE, HENRY | Halifax, Halifax Co. | 1866-1872 | (47, 50, 52) |
| BROWNE, HENRY, JR. | Halifax, Halifax Co. | 1866-1872 | (47, 50, 52) |
| BROWNE, H. & SONS | Halifax, Halifax Co. | 1871-1872 | (52) |
| BROWNE, H. | Bridgewater, Lunenburg Co. | 1890-1897 | (68) |
| BRYDEN, T. | Halifax, Halifax Co. | 1819 | |
| BRYMER, ALEXANDER | Halifax, Halifax Co. | 1866-1867 | (47) |
| CARR, JAMES | Halifax, Halifax Co. | 1863-1897 | (45, 47, 50-58, 68) |
| Advertises as successor to A. Troup in 1863. | | | |
| CARSON, HENRY | Halifax, Halifax Co. | 1866-1867 | (47) |
| CARSON, WILLIAM | Halifax, Halifax Co. | 1866-1867 | (47) |
| CARTER, ANDREW | Liverpool, Queens Co. | 1866-1867 | (47) |
| CARTER, ANDREW W. | Pictou, Pictou Co. | 1879-1880 | (69) |

| | | | |
|---|---|---|---|
| CLEMMENS, ISAAC | Shelburne, Shelburne Co. | 1786 | (8) |
| CLEVERDON, J. R. | Halifax, Halifax Co. | 1840 | |
| CLEVERDON, WM. H. | Halifax, Halifax Co. | 1878-1897 | (57, 58, 68) |
| COGSWELL, ROBERT | Halifax, Halifax Co. | 1869-1897 | (50-58, 68) |
| COHN, S. J. | Halifax, Halifax Co. | 1873-1881 | (53-58) |
| CORNELIUS, J. | Halifax, Halifax Co. | 1866-1881— | (47, 54-58) |
| CRAWFORD, ROBERT | Halifax, Halifax Co. | 1822 | |
| CRAWFORD, WILLIAM | Halifax, Halifax Co. | 1816-1867 | (14, 45, 47) |
| CROSSKILL, GEORGE F. | Halifax, Halifax Co. | 1878-1897 | (57, 58, 68) |
| DAVIDSON, ROBERT | Halifax, Halifax Co. | 1830 | |
| DAVIDSON & FELTUS | Halifax, Halifax Co. | 1890-1897 | (68) |
| DAVISE, ROBERT | Granville Township, Annapolis Co. | 1838 | (15) |
| DEAN, WILLIAM | Halifax, Halifax Co. | 1792-1793 | (9, 11) |
| DOYLE, PHILIP | Halifax, Halifax Co. | 1866-1867 | (47) |
| DRAVIS, HENRY | Halifax, Halifax Co. | 1866-1867 | (47) |
| EASTWOOD, JAMES | New Glasgow, Pictou Co. | 1879-1880 | (69) |
| ETTER, BENJAMIN | Halifax, Halifax Co. | 1787-1813 | (9, 11) |
| ETTER, PETER, JR. | Halifax, Halifax Co. & Fort Cumberland, in Westmorland Co., N.B. | 1782-1787 1787-1798 | (74) |
| ETTER, I. J. | Halifax, Halifax Co. | 1890-1897 | (68) |
| FLETCHER, W. S. | Pictou, Pictou Co. | 1840 | |
| FLETCHER, WILLIAM | Wallace, Cumberland Co. | 1866-1867 | (47) |
| GEDDES, CHARLES (1749-1810) | Halifax, Halifax Co. | 1783-1810 | (9, 11, 74) |

Worked in London, Boston, and New York before coming to Halifax.

| | | | |
|---|---|---|---|
| GEDDIE, JOHN (1778-1843) | Pictou, Pictou Co. | 1817-1843 | (15) |
| GLASGOW, H. & CO. | Halifax, Halifax Co. | 1873-1877 | (53-57) |
| GLASGOW, HENRY | Halifax, Halifax Co. | 1878-1879 | (57) |
| GORDON, THOMAS | Halifax, Halifax Co. | 1792-1793 | (9, 11) |
| GORDON, WILLIAM | New Glasgow, Pictou Co. | 1879-1880 | (69) |
| GREENE, JOHN | Dartmouth, Halifax Co. | 1876-1881 | (55-58) |
| GREENWOOD, SAMUEL M. | Halifax, Halifax Co. | 1815 | |
| GUEST, THOMAS | Yarmouth, Yarmouth Co. | 1866-1867 | (47) |
| HARPER, ALEXANDER | Halifax, Halifax Co. | 1813 | |
| HARDWICK, LESLIE | Annapolis Royal, Annapolis Co. | 1866-1867 | (47) |

| | | | |
|---|---|---|---|
| HERBIN, JOHN | Windsor, Hants Co. | 1866-1867 | (47) |
| | Halifax, Halifax Co. | 1871-1874 | (52, 53) |
| HUESTIS, G. A. | Windsor, Hants Co. | 1890-1897 | (68) |
| HUNTER, A. | Halifax, Halifax Co. | 1819 | |
| JOHNSON, THOS. C. | Halifax, Halifax Co. | 1863-1881 | (45, 47, 50-58) |
| JOHNSON, T. C. & SONS | Halifax, Halifax Co. | 1874 to present | |
| KEEN, JAMES | Digby, Digby Co. | 1866-1867 | (47) |
| KERR, HENRY M. | Halifax, Halifax Co. | 1863-1881 | (45-58) |
| LADD, .... .... | Amherst, Cumberland Co. | ?1835-1840? | |
| LANGILLE, J. A. | Acadia Mines, Colchester Co. | 1890-1897 | (68) |
| LEEDHAM, J. | Halifax, Halifax Co. | 1863 | (45) |
| LEIST, M. | Halifax, Halifax Co. | 1877-1879 | (56-58) |
| LEVY & MICHAELS<br>    Morris Levy.<br>    Abraham L. Michaels. | Halifax, Halifax Co. | 1876-1881 | (55-58) |
| LITHGOW, WILLIAM | Halifax, Halifax Co. | 1838-1852 | (14) |
| LITTLE, DAVID | Pictou, Pictou Co. | | |
| LLOYD, ANDREW J. | Halifax, Halifax Co. | 1866-1867 | (47) |
| MCALLISTER, GEORGE | Halifax, Halifax Co. | 1866-1881 | (47, 55-58) |
| MCCARTNEY, J. G. | Dartmouth, Halifax Co. | 1878-1881 | (57-58) |
| MCCULLOCH, JOHN | Halifax, Halifax Co. | 1844-1875 | (45, 47,<br>50-53, 74) |
| MCELMON, DAVID R. | Halifax, Halifax Co. | 1866-1867 | (47) |
| MCLELLAN, R. N. C. | Halifax, Halifax Co. | 1847 | |
| MALCOLM, JOHN | Windsor, Hants Co. | 1791, 1795 | (10) |
| MASTER, RICHARD | Halifax, Halifax Co. | 1838 | (14) |
| MARSTERS, R. U. | Halifax, Halifax Co. | 1817, 1826 | |
| MILLROSE, GEORGE | Chester Township,<br>    Lunenburg Co. | 1838 | (15) |
| MILLS, ANDREW | Halifax, Halifax Co. | 1816 | |
| MILLS, W. N. | Pictou, Pictou Co. | 1866-1880 | (47, 69) |
| MORGAN, CHARLES P. | Truro, Colchester Co. | 1890-1897 | (68) |
| MORGAN, GEORGE | Halifax, Halifax Co. | 1866-1872 | (47, 52) |
| MORGAN, JOHN | Halifax, Halifax Co. | 1869-1872 | (50-52) |
| MOSS, MYER "from London" | Truro, Colchester Co. | 1866-1867 | (47) |
| MOTT, CHARLES | Halifax, Halifax Co. | 1880-1881 | (58) |

| | | | |
|---|---|---|---|
| MUDIE, THOMAS | Halifax, Halifax Co. | 1807-1813 | |
| | Pictou, Pictou Co. | 1828 | |
| | Pictou, Pictou Co. | 1866-1867 | (47) |
| MULITORE, ALFRED | Halifax, Halifax Co. | 1866-1867 | (47) |
| MUNRO, THOMAS | New Glasgow, Pictou Co. | 1879-1880 | (69) |
| MURPHY, JOHN J. | Halifax, Halifax Co. | 1876-1881 | (55 58) |
| NEILSON, WM. | Halifax, Halifax Co. | 1838 | (14) |
| NEWMAN, W. H. | Halifax, Halifax Co. | 1863-1897 | (45, 50-58, 68) |

"Manufacturer and importer of fine jewellery and watches."

| | | | |
|---|---|---|---|
| PAGE, DAVID | Truro Township, Colchester Co. | 1838 | (15) |
| PAGET, JOHN | Halifax, Halifax Co. | 1783 | |
| REED, ISAAC | Shelburne, Shelburne Co. | 1786-1787 | (8) |
| RENWICK, GEORGE | Halifax, Halifax Co. | 1863-1874 | (45, 52, 53) |
| RENWICK, JAMES R. | Halifax, Halifax Co. | 1873-1874 | (53) |
| ROGERS, J. | Halifax, Halifax Co. | 1818 | |
| ROSS, ANGUS | New Glasgow, Pictou Co. | 1866-1867 | (47) |
| ROSS, J. | Halifax, Halifax Co. | 1818 | |
| ROSS, M. S. | Pictou, Pictou Co. | 1879-1880 | (69) |
| ROSS, WILLIAM, JR. | Pictou, Pictou Co. | 1879-1880 | (69) |
| ROSS, W. G. | Halifax, Halifax Co. | 1876-1878 | (55, 56) |
| ROSS, W. G. & CO. | Halifax, Halifax Co. | 1878-1881 | (57, 58) |
| SANCTON, JOHN | Bridgetown, Annapolis Co. | 1866-1867 | (47) |
| SCHAEFFER, HERMAN | Halifax, Halifax Co. | 1880 1881 | (58) |
| SHAPPS, OBADIAH | Amherst, Cumberland Co. | 1866-1867 | (47) |
| SIMPSON, DAVID | Pictou, Pictou Co. | 1866-1880 | (47-69) |
| SMITH, JOHN R. | Arichat, Richmond Co. | 1838 | (15) |
| SPIKE, THOMAS D. | Halifax, Halifax Co. | 1869-1881 | (50-58) |
| SPURR, THOMAS R. | Annapolis Township, Annapolis Co. | 1838 | (15) |
| STIRSKEY, F. | Halifax, Halifax Co. | 1873-1881 | (53-58) |
| STOUGHTON, DULCINA | Shelburne, Shelburne Co. | 1787-1788 | (8) |

Watch finisher.

| | | | |
|---|---|---|---|
| TAYLOR, THOMAS | Canning, Kings Co. | 1866-1867 | (47) |
| THOMPSON, W. | Halifax, Halifax Co. | 1863 | (45) |
| TOBIN, JOHN | Beaver River, Yarmouth Co. | 1847 | (40) |

Manufactured brass and wooden clock works.

| | | | |
|---|---|---|---|
| TROTT, G. | Halifax, Halifax Co. | 1866-1867 | (47) |
| TROUP, ALEXANDER, SR. (1776-1856) | Halifax, Halifax Co. | 1838-1856 | (14, 74) |

James Carr advertises as successor to late A. Troup in 1863.

| | | | |
|---|---|---|---|
| TROUP, ALEXANDER, JR. (1806-1873) | Halifax, Halifax Co. | 1838-1873 | (14, 45, 47, 50-53) |
| TROUP, THOMAS (1819-1877) | Halifax, Halifax Co. | 1869-1874 | (50-53, 74) |
| VOGEL, HERMAN | Halifax, Halifax Co. | 1869-1881 | (50-58) |
| WALLACE, ROBERT | Halifax, Halifax Co. | 1875-1881 | (54-58) |
| WARMUNDE, CHARLES | Halifax, Halifax Co. | 1873-1878 | (53-56) |
| WEATHERS, MICHAELS | Shelburne, Shelburne Co. | 1786 | (8) |
| WHITE, W. H. | Wolfville, Kings Co. | 1866-1867 | (47) |
| WILLIAMS, GEORGE | Halifax, Halifax Co. | 1866-1867 | (47) |
| YUILL, WILLIAM G. | Truro, Colchester Co. | 1866-1867 | (47) |

# Bibliography

*Manuscripts*

Assessment rolls, poll tax lists, census records, marriage bonds, church records, land grants, family histories and township books have all been rewarding sources of information concerning cabinetmakers. Inventories of property that had been filed with wills in the Court of Probate were valuable indications of the types of furniture owned at certain dates. The notes made by the late Harry Piers in the accession book of the Nova Scotia Museum of Science have been of great assistance, as has the paper on "Old Furniture Made in Nova Scotia" prepared by Florence Belcher Payzant for the Antiquarian Society of Halifax in 1939.

*Newspapers*

Many newspapers in the collection of the Public Archives of Nova Scotia have been consulted, particularly the *Royal Gazette* from 1789 to 1843, the *Acadian Recorder* and the *Nova Scotian* of Halifax, and the *Colonial Patriot* and the *Eastern Chronicle* of Pictou.

*Other Publications*

All the directories of Nova Scotia which I could find have been carefully searched for the names of cabinetmakers, but unfortunately many of these deal with Halifax alone. Belcher's and Cunnabell's almanacs have been consulted and some further information found in the catalogues and reports of provincial and international exhibitions which are in the Akins Library of the Nova Scotia Archives. County and local histories and genealogies have also been important for background and for details on furniture makers, especially those of Annapolis, Barrington, Bridgetown, Kings, Lunenburg and Pictou.

Akins, T. B.—*Selections from the Public Documents of the Province of Nova Scotia*. Halifax, N.S., 1869.

Bell, Winthrop Pickard, *The "Foreign Protestants" and the Settlement of Nova Scotia*. Toronto. University of Toronto Press, 1960.

Blakeley, Phyllis R., *Glimpses of Halifax 1867-1900*, Halifax, N.S. 1949 Publication No. 9 of Public Archives of Nova Scotia.

Blakeley, Phyllis R., "Music in Nova Scotia, 1605-1867," *Dalhousie Review*, Vol. 31, Nos. 2 and 3, Summer and Winter, 1951

Blakeley, Phyllis Ruth, *The Story of Nova Scotia*. Toronto, J. M. Dent & Sons, 1950.

Cameron, James M., *Industrial History of the New Glasgow District*. New Glasgow, 1960.

Campbell, George G., *The History of Nova Scotia*. Toronto, Ryerson Press, 1948.

Edwards, Major Joseph P., "The Shelburne that was and is not" and "Vicissitudes of a Loyalist City," *Dalhousie Review*, Vol. 2, Nos. 2 and 3, July and October, 1922.

Fergusson, C. Bruce, *Mechanics' Institutes in Nova Scotia*, Halifax, N.S., 1960. Bulletin No. 14 of the Public Archives of Nova Scotia.

Fisher, Edgar, "History of Bass River Furniture Chair Factory", in proceedings of the Colchester Historical Society, 1954-1957.

*Halifax and Its Business* . . . Halifax, Nova Scotia Printing Co., 1876.

145

Harvey, D.C., "The Intellectual Awakening of Nova Scotia," *Dalhousie Review*, Vol. 13, No. 1, April, 1933.

Heal, Sir Ambrose, *The London Furniture Makers from the Restoration to the Victorian Era*, 1660-1840. B. T. Batsford, London, 1953.

Kettell, Russell Hawes, *The Pine Furniture of Early New England*. New York. Dover Publishing Co., 1929.

Lockwood, Luke Vincent, *Colonial Furniture in America*, New York, Scribner's, 1901.

Macdonald, James S., *Annals of the North British Society*, Halifax, N.S., with portraits and biographical notes 1768 to 1903.

MacLaren, George, *The Pictou Book*. New Glasgow, N.S. 1954.

Martell, James S., *Immigration to and emigration from Nova Scotia, 1815-1838*. Publication No. 6 of the Public Archives of Nova Scotia. 1942.

Miller, Edgar G., *American Antique Furniture*, New York. M. Barrows & Co. 1936.

Piers, Harry, ed. *Biographical Review* of the leading citizens of the Province of Nova Scotia. Biographical Review Publishing Co. Boston, 1900.

Piers, Harry, & Mackay, Donald C., *Master Goldsmiths and Silversmiths of Nova Scotia and Their Marks*. The Antiquarian Club, Halifax, N.S. 1948.

Provincial Museum of Nova Scotia and Science Library, Reports, 1900-1939.

Public Archives of Nova Scotia, Halifax, N.S., Reports, 1931-1959.

Stevens, Gerald, *The Canadian Collector*. Toronto, Ryerson Press, 1957.

Wainwright, Kennedy B., *Our Story of Stewiacke and Shubenacadie*, a book of remembrance (1955) privately printed.